Courageous Career Change

Fearlessly Earn the Executive Role You Deserve

COURAGEOUS CAREER CHANGE

FEARLESSLY EARN

THE EXECUTIVE ROLE

YOU DESERVE

AMY L. ADLER, MBA

Copyright © 2020 Amy L. Adler. All rights reserved.

No portion of this book may be reproduced in any form without permission from the publisher, except as permitted by U.S. copyright law.

For permissions, visit:
www.fivestrengths.com
aadler@fivestrengths.com
https://linkedin.com/in/amyladler

ISBN: 979-8-56118-713-1

For my father.

CONTENTS

ACKNOWLEDGMENTS	XI
FOREWORD	XIII
INTRODUCTION	XV

PART 1 | PREPARE

CHAPTER 1 | WHERE DID THE LOVE GO? ... 3
- Is It Time to Move On? ... 3
- Mindful Movement ... 5

CHAPTER 2 | FIGHT THE FEAR ... 7
- "Fear Is the Mind-Killer" ... 7
- Ten Common Fears That Hold Back Career Growth ... 8
- Own Your Fear ... 9
- Dig Deep for Career Confidence ... 12
- Cut the Mental Clutter and Believe in Your Success ... 14

CHAPTER 3 | FOCUS YOUR INTENTIONS ... 17
- Run to a Brilliant Opportunity, Not Away from a Poor Fit ... 17
- Power Your Decision with the "Rule of Fives" ... 18
- Lead Your Career Change like You Would Lead Your Company ... 19
- Focus Your Transition Strategy ... 22
- A Strategy for Entrepreneurs ... 25
- What If You've Been Fired? ... 26
- Whom Can You Trust? ... 27

PART 2 | CRAFT

CHAPTER 4 | STOP WRITING YOUR RESUME ... 33
- There Is No Easy Path to Growth ... 33
- Your Search Does Not Start with Your Resume ... 34

CHAPTER 5 | STRATEGY FOR SUCCESS ... 37
- Focus Your Research ... 37
- Looking for Work Is Now Your Full-Time Job ... 45
- Be Efficient ... 46

CHAPTER 6 | PREPARE AN OUTSTANDING RESUME — 49
- Why Build a Resume? — 49
- Why Does Your Resume Drive Your Interview? (It Is Not What You Think) — 50
- Crafting the Best Resume for You and Your Unique Job Search — 51
- Show Pride and Humility in Your Resume — 53
- Resume versus Job Application: What's the Difference? And Why Does It Matter? — 55
- Resume Sections That Matter to Hiring Executives — 56
- Resume Design Strategies — 71
- Resume Length — 73
- Proofread! — 75

CHAPTER 7 | WRITING AN EXCEPTIONAL COVER LETTER — 77
- Cover Letters Are Crucial — 77
- Never Send a Naked Resume — 78
- Qualities of a Great Cover Letter — 79
- Cover Letter Templates Fail — 80
- Don't Miss an Opportunity to Use Your Cover Letter Effectively — 81
- Format of a Great Cover Letter — 81
- Sample Resumes and Cover Letters — 83

CHAPTER 8 | EXECUTIVE RESUME WRITING FOR ENTREPRENEURS — 85
- Constructing Your Story for the Corporate World — 85
- How to Approach Your Resume When You're an Entrepreneur — 86
- The Executive Biography — 88
- What If You Failed as an Entrepreneur? Where Does That Go on Your Resume? — 90

CHAPTER 9 | WORKING WITH A RESUME WRITING SERVICE — 91
- How to Choose an Executive Resume Writing Service — 91
- Why Choose a Resume Writer? You Don't Know What You Know about Yourself — 96

PART 3 | NETWORK

CHAPTER 10 | CONNECT FOR SUCCESS — 101
- Job Seekers Succeed when They Network — 101
- How Your Inside Connection Leads to Your Next Executive Role — 103
- Measure Your Job Search Networking Success — 106

CHAPTER 11 | LINKEDIN — 109
- Key Reasons for an Optimized LinkedIn Profile — 109
- Profile Keyword Strategy — 111
- Do These Ten Things on LinkedIn Right Now—All in Less than One Hour — 112
- Write a Great LinkedIn Headline — 113
- Join Groups to Boost Your Relevance — 114
- Choose the Right LinkedIn Groups for Your Executive Job Search — 115
- Key Metrics for Your LinkedIn Profile — 115
- Accept (Almost All) LinkedIn Connection Requests — 117
- The Five People You Need to Know on LinkedIn — 119
- Third-Degree Connections Matter — 121
- Becoming a LION: Balancing the Pros and Cons — 123
- Why Your Profile Is Not Your Resume — 125
- Protect Your Profile — 127

PART 4 | APPLY

CHAPTER 12 | THE TACTICAL SEARCH — 131
- Apply for Only Six Jobs — 131
- Stop Scouring Online Job Boards — 132
- The Informational Interview: What It Is, What It Isn't, and How to Do It — 134
- Cool Tools to Search for Jobs Online — 136
- Use a Customer Relationship Management Tool — 138

CHAPTER 13 | WORKING WITH RECRUITERS — 141
- Recruiters Do Not Work with Job Seekers — 141
- Etiquette Tips for Working with Recruiters — 143

CHAPTER 14 | THE INTERVIEW — 147
- There Is No Such Thing as "Not Part of the Interview" — 147
- Prepare for Your Interview Success — 149
- Interview Persuasively — 151
- Practicing Your Pitch — 154
- Winning the Interview Game — 155
- Interview Mistakes That Will Sabotage Your Chances — 157
- Body Language for Your Telephone Interview — 159
- Presentation for Your Video Interview — 160
- Cracking the Office Dress Code — 161
- Finish the Interview by Thanking the Interviewing Team — 164

CONCLUSION — 167
- Measure Your Success by the Offers You Reject — 167

ACKNOWLEDGMENTS

My first career was in book publishing, so producing my own book from this side of the keyboard was both familiar and strange to me. Knowing all the steps to producing a book is not the same as writing one, and the writing is not a process I could have undertaken alone:

To my mother and father, thank you for always telling me that I could.

To Jessica and Sarah, thank you for letting me show you that you can be a mom, a business owner, and anything else you want to be.

To Doug, my biggest champion and my truest love, thank you for your vocal and constant support for my career (not to mention this project). You are an unmitigated source of strength.

FOREWORD

DR. LEO BUSCAGLIA ONCE OPINED that "the past is a cancelled check, the future a promissory note, and the present is cash in hand." How true. The present is all we truly have.

Making the decision to go through with career change is a stressful process within itself. Sometimes we know in our mind and heart that it's time for a change, but for various reasons, we hesitate. This empowering book focuses on the critical considerations of the job search. Amy Adler helps bring organization to what is all too often an ineffectual and frustrating process. In so many ways, this book can serve as a framework to take inventory, focus on your intentions, and realize that fear is not unfounded but instead can be overcome with the right strategies as you navigate the complexities of seeking a new role.

I'm a firm believer that the right people come into your life at the right time. From the moment I spoke with Amy, there was an immediate connection and a sense that I had finally met someone who could not just help pragmatically prepare and navigate an executive job search but identify something much deeper. Beyond any leader, colleague or mentor, she forced me to consider the *why* and the *what*. Why was I yearning for change? What was my motivation? Eventually, our work together allowed me to not only answer the larger philosophical questions but also, more importantly, to create a cohesive narrative for my own career path. In fact, Amy's strategies, many detailed in this book, were pivotal in my own transformation from a prestigious 150-plus-year-old brand to an exciting adventure with a 12-year-old Silicon Valley fintech company.

Courageous Career Change is a must-have guide for any job seeker—it takes what can be extremely daunting and provides a practical approach to prepare, navigate and successfully manage your journey. Amy has shared her rich history and wisdom—along with years of experience supporting countless executives and other professionals in achieving their career aspirations—to create a blueprint for success that is second to none.

Victor Ingalls
Global Fintech Executive

INTRODUCTION

To misquote Paul Simon's "Kodachrome," I don't remember a lot of what I learned in high school. Significantly, however, I do remember learning of Maslow's hierarchy of needs—it's a concept that has always resonated with me.

Briefly, Maslow showed that at the most basic level, we need food, clothing, shelter, and all the fundamental things that enable our bodies to survive. At the highest level, we self-actualize or reach our full potential. In the realm of your executive career, your joy in your work is your self-actualization.

We are at our best when we love what we do; that should come as no surprise. I'm sure there have been many moments in your career that sparked a smile on your face, not to mention accolades from your team or boss. In aggregate, that's your personal definition of career-related joy.

The harder questions are these: How do you make those moments happen more often and more predictably? And what do you do when they don't happen at all?

This book will guide you through the maze that is your executive career change, providing tips and tactics to secure an interview for a role in your ideal company. We'll explore how to write a professional, polished, and winning resume, LinkedIn profile, and cover letter; how to form productive networks that get results; and how to use processes and resources to propel you successfully and joyfully into the next phase of your career.

PART 1

PREPARE

—1—
WHERE DID THE LOVE GO?

IS IT TIME TO MOVE ON?

SINCE YOU'RE READING THIS BOOK, you're likely taking a hard look at your career—weighing the pros and cons of leaving your current job or transitioning to a new position or industry. Maybe you're out of work and need help refreshing your resume or prepping your interview skills. You might be testing the water in the employment market or bringing yourself up to speed with present-day skills, talents, and education. Whatever the situation, if you can answer yes to any or all of the following questions, you've likely lost the joy you deserve in your career.

- Are you dissatisfied with your company's trajectory?
- Do you wish you could earn a promotion or better compensation faster?
- Are you unsure your industry is the right one for you?
- If you had no obstacles, would you immediately change industries or job functions to ones you've already thought about?
- Do you dread Monday mornings?

Even professionals with ten, twenty, or more years' experience can face a crossroads in their careers. Your answers to the above could be all it takes to trigger a move, but there might be other factors in play.

Have You Upskilled with a New Degree or Valuable Certificate?

If you are midway or further into your professional career, and you have just finished a bachelor's or master's degree or other specialized certification, a role change could take advantage of your newfound expertise. Perhaps it's time to leave your old post and industry behind and move forward with the new.

Are You at the Logical End of a Career Path?

I've worked with many people who reached the senior executive level in their field and realized they didn't have much to add to their current role. As one executive put it, "I don't know what I want to do next; I just know that it's not what I've been doing for the last twenty years." If this sounds like you, perhaps you could explore a high-potential, if lesser, role in a different industry.

Is It the Industry or Your Company?

There is a vast difference between being bored in your company and being bored with your industry. There is always another company to explore if your current place of work does not provide you with the right challenges. Tease apart the sense of ennui you feel related to your current company and its opportunities (or lack thereof) and the perception that you have maxed out your industry.

Are You Discouraged by the Lack of Growth Projected for Your Industry?

Growth patterns in every sector change, and some industries die out in favor of those offering better technology or improved solutions. Yours might be in a period of contraction, much as the housing and construction market did in the early 2000s. If you can see the handwriting on the wall and the future of your current industry appears dismal, then take some time to evaluate your role in it. If you can't see yourself in a viable industry two, five, or even ten years down the road, then perhaps it is time for you to explore new options.

When Shouldn't I Change My Career or Industry?

If you are having a rough time of it in your current company, you might feel compelled to toss the baby out with the bathwater and escape your industry altogether. While I would never suggest you stay in a toxic environment, you might find that it is not the industry you can't abide but rather your current company. If you truly appreciate so much of what your industry has to offer, then take time to test your options and explore other companies in your field. You might find that the work powers you, but you need a fresh environment in which to do it.

MINDFUL MOVEMENT

Long-Term Career Success versus Instant Gratification

The term "career" reflects the series of jobs you hold over some time. In the cases of most executives, their industry, promotions, network, and drive will link these positions. I posit that a vision for the long term will serve a savvy executive better than a scattershot approach of moving whimsically from position to position.

B. F. Skinner's Rat in the Box

We all recall the Skinner box with the rat—the rat presses a bar, and at various intervals the behavior produces a treat for the rat. The process ultimately trains the rat to press the bar frantically when it delivers the reward only infrequently. You could find yourself in the same trap if you keep thinking your next career will be better than the one you have now. Sometimes it is better, but not always, and that's what keeps you moving from job to job and target to target. If instability matched with excitement and inconsistent reward is the stimulation your career path needs, then you can make it happen.

The downside is that eventually the process will burn out, and you'll be left with a resume showing a clear history of job-hopping to support you when you get serious about your career.

"The Millionaire Next Door"

In *The Millionaire Next Door*, Thomas J. Stanley writes that the unassuming millionaire drives an older car, dresses normally, spends little, and stays on the same career path—if not in the same job—for decades. The successful executive in this scenario might not be the flashiest on the outside, but he or she is the solid, trustworthy, promotable leader on whom the executive board can always rely. The path to this success doesn't have to be boring or staid, but it is likely to be established on a steady, gradual incline rather than a series of bumps, jiggles, and jumps. This executive will usually hold a solid resume showing a few related positions over several years or decades.

Rat or Millionaire?

In an employment marketplace that allows you to focus on any goal you can imagine, will you be the rat in the Skinner box, focusing on short-term indulgence, or will you be the millionaire next door? What if you have been slowly and steadily rising for years, and you are absolutely ready for a change? Will your network or a potential hiring executive see you as flighty and inconsistent? The choice is yours, but ideally, you'll choose the path that suits your long-term goals while creating essential career satisfaction.

— 2 —

FIGHT THE FEAR

"FEAR IS THE MIND-KILLER"

Fans of *Dune* by Frank Herbert will remember that famous quote. Equally memorable is "A beginning is a very delicate time."

One of the clearest markers that you are ready to leave your current company and join a new one is simply the knowledge that you can do more or better in another environment. Once you have come to this decision, however, you might struggle with your motivations, your need to elevate your income, or your commitment to the incredible team you have created. These fears are natural because we all fear change. The status quo is a known quantity, whereas moving toward something new, even if it's what you really want, can provoke anxiety even in the most accomplished of executives.

If you are looking for a clear reason to leave, you can always find one. But if you're looking for a *smart* reason to leave, you need to face a few key fears that most people in career transition experience.

TEN COMMON FEARS THAT HOLD BACK CAREER GROWTH

Businesspeople I have coached through complex career changes are among the strongest, most fearless individuals I have met in my career. They lead large teams. They put innovative products to market. They guide budgets in the millions, if not hundreds of millions. In a word, they are powerful, interesting individuals who overcome meaningful professional challenges every day.

Whether these executives know exactly what they are seeking in a new role, or whether they are truly exploring the many options before them, these daring leaders often share many fears about the career change process. If your blood pressure rises slightly at the thought of one or more of these common fears, you're certainly not alone, as unique as your career situation might be.

Fears about Making a Move

1. Fear of having to make a choice to leave a "good enough" situation at work.
2. Fear of walking the career transition journey alone, without someone with whom you can be brutally honest.
3. Fear of adding more stress to days that already have twenty-five hours of distractions.
4. Fear of having to network to find the right role—especially for introverts.
5. Fear of adding ONE. MORE. THING. to today's to-do list.
6. Fear of writing a resume (or the gnawing feeling that you don't have the right resume).
7. Fear of having the boss find out (note: your LinkedIn profile doesn't have to announce it).

Fears about Not Making a Move

8. Fear of showing up to the same job again on Monday.
9. Fear of wasting time by inaction today.

10. Fear that the right job is out there waiting for you, but someone else snagged it first.

Do any of these resonate? I would guess that if none strikes a chord, you're not ready to engage in a career transition—you haven't thought deeply about how their answers inform your wants and needs in a future career. Without that analysis, you will continue to be successful, but you won't be as insightful about your process as you could be. Neither will you challenge yourself to grow.

If your blood pressure is just a little higher now than it was before starting this chapter, then now is an opportunity for you to find real clarity about your goals and fearlessly seek and achieve the executive career opportunities that you know are right for you.

OWN YOUR FEAR

There is nothing easy about career change. The path can have some surprising turns, but almost always, these new explorations can lead to real insight. As executive career coaches, we see how, with self-exploration, executives experiencing career change identify truths about their needs, goals, and career targets.

However, we also see those individuals afraid of seeing something new inside themselves. They are most often blustery, willing to take all the credit, and unlikely to peel back the layers to their own fears to uncover what worries them about the career change process.

Who remembers *Broadcast News*, a movie from the late 1980s? Jane's the quintessential brilliant Type A reporter, Tom is a pretty face for TV news, and Paul Moore is the station executive. If you remember the movie, you might also remember this quote from it:

Paul Moore: It must be nice to always believe you know better, to always think you're the smartest person in the room.

Jane Craig: No. It's awful.

And Jane certainly means it. The character is "right" so often that she forgets how to be wrong. She's so afraid of being overlooked, even though she's brilliant by any definition, she's abrasive.

What if the movie went a different way? What if Jane openly agreed that her path to growth was difficult—and she acknowledged that she had genuine concerns about her ability to be successful? When executives in career transition face the fact that they might have to be vulnerable—in conversations with their coaches, in interviews, in career contract negotiations—they are likely to find that people are more than willing to help them. They'll also find that being open about their fears doesn't define them as incompetent or unlikeable. In fact, they might find just the opposite—that acknowledging their fears about a career switch makes them seem more open to learning new things and more personable.

Are You Hiding Your Fear?

Fear is rarely an acceptable topic of conversation among extremely well-positioned executive leaders; evidently, the executive team should be stoic, proud, and fearless. But behind every executive title is an actual human being, with his or her own attitudes—and fears.

You know that as an executive you should portray fearlessness every day, so you might quietly stew about your job search. You may have many reasons for delaying action on it. For example, the holidays are coming, and you need to maintain some stability. Your spouse is also in transition. You're in the middle of an exciting—or draining—series of projects at work. Your team is counting on you. Your boss is counting on you. Your company is counting on you. Perhaps you have made tentative overtures into exploring the market. Either way, you're probably in a relatively balanced state of ambivalence—not enough pressure from either side to force a decision.

Perhaps this ambivalence comes from the fact that your reasons for staying in your current role have nothing to do with your specific needs. Does that mean you think (or I think) that you are a fearful person, or that you treat every challenge to improve your situation as an opportunity to retreat? Of course not. You wouldn't be in the position you are in right now if you rejected chances to grow and change and lead in your industry. Based on the profiles of the executives I have worked with in the past, I would venture to say that you are:

- extremely good at what you do

- ready to fight for what your company, your industry, or your team needs
- well-known as an excellent leader and mentor
- humble and willing to give your team credit rather than take it yourself

Moreover, you probably don't want to rock the boat in which you are standing. But you have to think about your career in terms of your individual needs and requirements for growth.

Give Yourself Some Thought

Your feelings about going to work every day in your executive role may range from genuine excitement to straight-up dread. But the job is yours to love or hate, and you may feel very protective of it. You wouldn't let anyone disparage you or your company, so you block yourself from scrutiny that might reveal its imperfections. Because you know how to do your job better than anyone else, you might think moving to another position would diminish your level of comfort in your role. I venture to guess that you have not shrunk from other types of challenges, so I strongly urge you to consider whether the unfamiliar is bad for you, and, conversely, whether the familiar is good.

I would encourage you to ask yourself the following questions. They are not easy questions to answer, but your responses might surprise you—either in a good or frustrating way.

- Do I answer every one of the challenges above with "Yes, but . . ."?
- Am I sure that what I have in my current executive role is the best situation for me? (It might be, but you have to evaluate it to be certain.)
- Am I afraid that change means failure?
- Am I afraid that I might not have the experience or know-how to succeed outside of my current organization?

These points may help you identify and perhaps confront fears that could hold you back in your career shift. This is not an indictment of your capability or your willingness to rise to every challenge that confronts you on a professional level; it's an opportunity to examine your mindset and thought processes as you step forward into unknown territory.

DIG DEEP FOR CAREER CONFIDENCE

An executive job search is one of the hardest things that you will ever do, and it can leave you feeling battered and bruised. Rejection for interviews or placements can hit your confidence hard. Instead of focusing on the discouragement, work on changing your perspective.

Career Confidence and Soul-Searching

Career confidence is that deep-seated feeling that you are an expert. You know you have what it takes to deliver what your executive team and your customers are seeking.

You will never get to a sense of career confidence, however, without some serious soul-searching. This sense of expertise matched with well-being can come only from an honest evaluation of yourself and your accomplishments.

Questions you should ask yourself:

- What benefit do I provide my current/past employers?
- What problems do I typically solve?
- What is my biggest career accomplishment?
- How do I know that I got it right with a customer or stakeholder?
- What has my current career portfolio (executive resume, LinkedIn, cover letter, executive biography, and so on) achieved for me? To what extent do I believe it is a powerful representation of my overall history?

Now go back and answer these questions again. Leave off the single-phrase answers you might have offered yourself—these are just your starting points. Amplify them. Expand on the problems you face, the specific excellence that you bring to the table, and the powerful outcomes you have delivered. Because you are an executive, these might be page-long expansions of a complex scenario with many moving parts.

Adjust Your Mindset

As you prepare to conduct your executive job search, you might be without a job but previously employed or have a job and want a change. Decades ago, people would start with one company and retire from that same company. In today's world, people change jobs or even careers many times throughout their lives. Factors such as corporate reorganizations, mergers, technology changes, and increased performance expectations have influenced an expansion of the job search market. Add in introduction of the gig economy, introduction of new technologies across virtually every industry, and structural changes due to the COVID pandemic, and we now see that the marketplace is a much more fluid environment in which the old rules will never again apply. When you keep your career mindset in "the old days," you are inviting every other applicant for your ideal job to overtake you.

These are all external factors to your job search, but it's the change in your internal mindset that can really affect your success. There are several approaches that you can take in adjusting your attitude and raising your confidence to win that brilliant job opportunity.

1. Look at the big picture. Jot down what works well and not so well for you. Focus on what you are good at and work to improve your weaker points. Many companies coach their employees to play to their strengths, for the greater success of the entire team. Take this approach in your executive job search.

2. Ask others. Reach out to those who know you well or have worked with you in the past. Ask for their perspective on skills or attributes that they have noticed in you.

3. Use your skills. Maintain your skill set. Keep current by using your skills either through volunteering or continuing education. When you are not up to date, you risk doubting that you are still up to the task.

4. Practice interviewing. Research and record a list of potential interview questions and practice with a trusted person. You will find yourself more at ease during an interview if you are prepared. Review your executive resume to brush up on your own history, so you can answer interview questions with confidence.

5. Keep involved with your network. Your network is the key to your finding a new executive position. Not only will you keep up on your industry, but you also might discover job opportunities that become available.

CUT THE MENTAL CLUTTER AND BELIEVE IN YOUR SUCCESS

Celebrate the things you do succeed in, knowing that faith in yourself might be all it takes to actualize success.

Visualize Your Success

Even if it sounds corny, visualizing your success can change your mindset. I don't believe that if you simply *will* something to happen, then you control the outcome. But I am a great believer in decluttering your mental cache of *musts* and *have tos*, so you have the space to create your success. From an executive job search perspective, this might mean delegating a few minutes at the beginning or end of your day to make that phone call to a connection who just might be the one to help. For others, going for a run or taking the dog on a long walk to nowhere to clear your head and give yourself a mental vacation might be just the thing to recharge your mind.

Accentuate the Positive; Eliminate the Negative

One of the hardest mental hurdles to overcome is not letting the one rotten thing that spoiled your week crowd out the dozens of times when you saved the day or made someone's job easier or brightened their morning with a kind word. We have a terrible tendency to let the one mishap of the week destroy our self-confidence and our self-image. Don't let the ever-present devil on your shoulder tell you what to think about yourself. Remember the good that you do and the successes you create—personally and professionally. Make a written list and post it on your monitor if you have to.

Recognize When You Fall Short—It's an Opportunity to Build Yourself Up

Nobody's perfect, and sometimes you will fall short of your goals. Maybe you feel you didn't quite get through to a networking contact. Perhaps you didn't apply for a choice position before the deadline. Maybe you let your executive job search go for a week or two while you handled some pressing issues that couldn't wait.

These things happen, but don't beat yourself up over them. Instead, try to do a ten-second gap analysis between what you did and what you, with 20/20 hindsight, wish you had done. Maybe you need to refine your marketing message or elevator pitch so you come across with more power and precision when you next reach out to a connection. Perhaps you need to put all of your job search deadlines in a private calendar on your phone, complete with twenty-four-hour reminders to keep you on task. Maybe you have to put some "give" in your schedule because your career is demanding, and you can't possibly be in two places at once every day of your week.

Allow Yourself Some Breathing Room

Take some time to regroup, get your calendar in order, and create a plan you feel good about. The first item on your list should always be permission to forgive yourself if you're not speeding through your job search. The rest of your list should focus on the ways you can build yourself up by creating achievable short-term actions. In this way, you'll find that the few small workable tasks that push you through your search will ultimately propel you into the executive career satisfaction you need.

— 3 —

FOCUS YOUR INTENTIONS

RUN TO A BRILLIANT OPPORTUNITY, NOT AWAY FROM A POOR FIT

You may be so desperate to get out of your job that you're willing to try any opportunity to escape. Perhaps you wouldn't call yourself desperate, but you may not be thinking clearly. If you cringe at the thought of spending one more day at your desk, if you regret taking on your current role, or if you'll take any reasonable offer to get out, slow down, take a breath, and pause.

Stop Fighting

I'm not suggesting you stop looking for a new role; I'm recommending you stop fighting your current situation and focus your thinking and strategy on the right way to exit your company into a career that is the best fit.

The worst thing you can do is telegraph that you are trying to leave. It's bad for your company, bad for your relationships at work, and a terrible mindset for you to embrace. You also risk taking a role you'll dislike as much as the one you have now by accepting a lower-level position just for the income or taking a job that fulfills a short-term goal but compromises long-term career satisfaction.

Run toward the Best Career Fit

Start developing a strategic plan that turns your thinking outward to identify what's next for you. By assessing what you want in a career—perhaps simply the opposite of what you have now—you create a set of fluid criteria that will guide your search. You'll position yourself to run toward the right role, and on the day when you finally separate from your current company, you can joyfully move forward into the executive career you dreamed of.

Imagine the satisfaction in that!

POWER YOUR DECISION WITH THE "RULE OF FIVES"

As discussed in chapter 2, fear is the one thing that can hold you back from switching careers. Like so many others who contemplate change, you might wonder if you *really* want to do something different. Do you agonize over how you'll leave your team and what you'll tell them? Do you question whether a new job will be any better than your current one? And if your work is so busy, how can you decide when a dozen problems compete for your attention? When will it ever be the right time?

Overload and fear can prevent an executive who is wise about their company from being wise about their career.

Decide either Today or in Five Days

Your decision is less complicated than you think. In fact, the only decision you have to make is *whether* to explore new career options. Focusing on the choice—to do or not to do—simplifies the vast universe of questions and unknowns that cause conflict and create mental noise.

Challenge yourself to decide if *today* is the right day to change your mindset. If you think your calendar is too full and you can't determine if today is the day to pursue a career change, then you've made a valid decision. You've taken the issue off the table, and you can reschedule your decision and the strategy for it for five days from now. Put it on your calendar and don't think about it for the next five days. Come back to it when you're fresh.

Be Accountable to Yourself

In your decision to move ahead, hold yourself accountable for the choices you make. You can do this in many small ways, assigning quantifiable metrics to each, so you know whether you've completed a task satisfactorily. By following the "Rule of Fives," you'll have amassed significant information and strategies that will inform and drive your executive career change.

Complete These Tasks Using the "Rule of Fives"

- Collect your annual reviews from the last five years.
- Reinvigorate your network and add five new members each week.
- Comment on five LinkedIn group posts each week (or each day if you're ambitious).
- Research in depth five companies each week you find interesting.
- Read five articles in your industry's top news sources.
- Call five people in your network with whom you've not spoken in five months.

LEAD YOUR CAREER CHANGE LIKE YOU WOULD LEAD YOUR COMPANY

I once saw a meme that read:

Executive 1: "What if we invest in our workforce, and they leave?"

Executive 2: "What if we don't, and they stay?"

Whoever rightly deserves the credit for this social media cartoon designed this to incite executives to invest in their company's talent. I don't believe there's an executive out there who thinks ignoring the needs of their workforce is wise. You probably agree with me.

Despite the axiomatic value of investing in the talent and expertise of their company, so many executives refuse to do the same for themselves—adamantly refusing to treat their own career growth with the same care and insightfulness. This lack of preparation and investment manifests in several ways:

- A loss of passion for their work while still trudging the same paths.
- Failing to create a thoughtful business plan for the success of their careers.
- Neglecting to build a career plan "inventory" with a compelling current resume, recognizable branding, or an engaging social media presence.
- Abandoning warm contacts once they've secured a position, assuming networking is a goal-specific strategy with little value once the ink dries on a contract.
- Failing to budget for the right consultants to guide them in making complex career decisions.

These executives are smart and insightful; they don't go down these paths on purpose. What starts as benign neglect quickly turns to outright apathy. The pattern disintegrates into a painful lack of motivation and career subsistence. They are unhappy in their roles, and they know they can do better, but they do nothing because change is too daunting. Fortunately, mastering the enterprise known as your career is not as complicated as running your company—although the personal stakes are infinitely greater.

Commit to Yourself

Executives who seek my help have one thing in common—they are all deeply committed to making their companies as successful as possible. They strategize and plan and execute, all with amazing results. What strikes me is that often they did not do the same with their careers. They worked hard, got promoted, got recruited, and got hired. Now their career trajectory has changed, they must plan to be successful, just as they planned for their companies to succeed.

Nothing Purposeful Happens on Its Own

While serendipity is great, the current employment marketplace for executive leaders shares only a passing similarity to those of the past. Executives need to focus on making purposeful change, which comes only out of purposeful decision making. So, ask yourself these questions:

1. What choices can I make today to improve my access to the right positions?
2. With whom do I need to speak to get my career change on track?
3. What are the resources I need to enact a positive career change?

These are the same questions you might ask your own corporate team about their decision-making processes.

Examine All the "Departments" in Your Career Change "Company"

Now break down your answers into their essential parts, perhaps by business department:

- Strategy (What is next for me?)
- Finance (What are my financial goals?)
- Accounting (What happens if I quit today?)
- Business development (Whom do I need to meet?)
- Marketing (How will I promote myself? What is my messaging?)
- Advertising and public relations (What documents do I need to promote my marketing message?)
- Operations (How will I keep track of and measure my progress? What are the most efficient processes I can implement?)

As you contemplate the choices you need to make, think about the resources you might use to create the greatest success in the shortest time. In the "Company" analogy, your business might require a marketing leader with expertise outside of your team's core competencies to attack a fresh market. Or perhaps a new financial strategist to build a well-researched acquisition plan. Certainly, if your company needed this expertise, you would source it. Wouldn't you do the same for your own career and invite a specialist to dedicate themselves to your success?

FOCUS YOUR TRANSITION STRATEGY

If you're so entrenched in the everyday minutiae of your current job, you may not have time to devote to a career shift—it's too overwhelming, too abstract, and you're just too busy finishing tasks A, B, and C before deadlines 1, 2, and 3. Prevent career-search paralysis by breaking your strategy down into workable chunks.

Set Manageable Goals Today

The first item on your career change agenda should be "Set Manageable Goals Today." Stop what you are doing, take a pen and paper, and create a list of all the things you wished your current executive role did for you or all the things it does that you love. Remember, delaying your decision to make a choice is also a choice. Make sure that any procrastination is for the right reasons, not because choosing to act is too hard.

Now examine this list:

- Are these rewards possible in your current job? If not, what executive role might you be targeting next?

- Are these ideal factors achievable in a reasonable time frame, assuming you put a reasonable amount of resources toward achieving them?

- Are you empowered to achieve these goals? If not, who can help you reach these goals?

Devise Several Sets of Plans to Achieve Your Goals

The second item on your executive career change agenda is to look critically at the goals you just established and think broadly about how you will layer your plans to accomplish them.

For example, if one of your goals for job satisfaction is to lead a larger team, does that mean your current company needs to hire more people (an internal business decision)? Or do you need to look outside your company for a role that gives you this opportunity? If the former, with whom should you speak to build a business case to grow your team? If the latter, what executive job offer would be so compelling that you couldn't ignore it? Can you define this role more clearly? If you can define it, are you ready to set that level of change in motion? Knowing how you will plan for various outcomes of your research can help you establish a series of steps that won't overwhelm your busy schedule.

Overall, plan for your career change in several layers—what you can do today, what you can achieve in the medium term, and what you need to do to ensure that you reach your long-term goals. Think about what you can do on your own to achieve your goals and what will require you to involve others who can support your goal-achievement strategy.

Make Note of Your Career Wins

Keep track of your own career successes. When you need to report on them in your annual reviews, you can discuss your accomplishments easily. Your manager may not remember every detail of your major projects, but your annual self-assessment and formal review will act as reminders. By keeping track of your successes, you're helping your leadership evaluate you effectively. In the best scenario, your manager will use this material to help you rise to the next career level, but this body of knowledge about you will also support your career change goals. If you hire an executive resume writer and career coach, they will use this information to create your career portfolio. In addition, these successes form the meat of the answers you will give during job interviews—having a record of your successes at your fingertips will make the process much easier and more comfortable.

You might not recognize that these wins are the kinds of things you, as an executive, do every day. You probably don't think of them as successes because you are accustomed to delivering superior results in everything you do. Nevertheless, recording your accomplishments is necessary to support your future promotions, job transfers, and selection for major new projects that can advance your career.

If you are a senior executive with an office in the C-suite, then you might find measuring your successes to be difficult. Likely, you are not performing every single task for which your division has oversight. You might have ten or twenty or one hundred people reporting to you and working on various aspects of widely distributed and complex projects. If you can break the projects your team is completing down into major sections, then you can explain in several formats how your leadership directly affects the project success and its effects on your company's bottom line.

Use a Spreadsheet

Your project managers may have already delivered their project milestones and timelines. If you can input these into a spreadsheet, you can also mark your own successes and leadership contributions to each project. Place a milestone list down the left-hand side and put headers across the top such as "team members," "budget," "key obstacles," "solutions developed," "deliverables," and any other measurables you believe are relevant to your company's growth. The more you can provide calculable, quantifiable results, with dollars earned, dollars saved, percentages of increase or decrease of important metrics, and any other key performance indicators (KPIs) that matter most to your company, the better prepared you will be to report on your successes when the time comes to evaluate your own performance.

Use a Word Processing File

Sometimes, the successes you need to record are best maintained in a word processing document. Treat these personal files as narratives of your ongoing successes. Record elements of each project that you found easy, the ones you found challenging, and the specific strategies you used to make sure that each project was a success. Keep copies of these files on your personal home computer, rather than your work computer, so you can be honest with yourself and maintain records that are accurate from a professional standpoint and a psychological one.

Use Document Scans

Files you may have access to only once or twice per year include evaluations by your board or your executive team. If your company permits, keep copies of these records somewhere you can access them easily and quickly. Scan them in to keep track of the exact comments your superiors make about your work successes. Also keep scanned copies of any letters from customers, vendors, or professional associates. Often, what people say about you carries more weight than what you can say about yourself—and serves as a great memory jog when you have to deliver concrete evidence of your top-notch performance.

Nobody Can Do It for You, but You Can Always Ask for Help

There is nobody as invested in your career as you are, so while *you* must take charge of your executive career transition to turn organic growth into planned executive success, you can always ask for judicious advice from the right sources. As you look at the choices you must make, start to think about the resources you will need to create the greatest success in the shortest amount of time.

A STRATEGY FOR ENTREPRENEURS

As the economy fluctuates, many entrepreneurs take stock of their lengthy careers and successes in the companies they built. We hear of high-tech leaders who built companies from their basement and manufacturing leaders who built product suites appealing to the mass market. If you are an entrepreneur with a company that has potentially maxed it out its life cycle or is about to be sold, you might consider joining the paid workforce as an employee in another company. The following strategies can help you build a transition plan.

Define Your Network

Of course, as an entrepreneur, you know lots of people. You meet them in business meetings, in your Chamber of Commerce, through friends, and through friends of friends. But have you ever approached any of them with critical business questions? It's even less likely that you've mentioned your own career advancement. Now is the time to revive old relationships. Building a list of people to call to discuss opportunities in other companies and industries is an essential, if sometimes challenging, part of the process.

Assess Your Own Skill Set

As an entrepreneur, you likely wear many hats. Depending on the fire you are putting out, you might be CFO, CEO, or CIO on any given day. You might also be sales executive, human resources executive, or the guy who has to run to the hardware store to pick up a new light switch. Other entrepreneurs would sympathize with how thinly you have been stretched. They would also understand that you might find it hard to identify the skills you could build on in a new role.

Take an hour or two to write down what you love about your job, what you hate about it, and where your skills fit in to what you want to be doing next. If you don't know where your assets might be of value in a corporate environment, speak with an expert, such as an executive career consultant, who can help you make that determination.

Prepare Your Resume and Career Portfolio

If you know exactly what you want to be doing in a new company, now is the time to have your executive resume prepared. If you are still in decision-making mode, go back to number 2 on this list—preparing yourself for a new career but taking the steps out of order will only result in your mounting frustration.

As you do the research, you'll learn what goes into a resume for a former entrepreneur that resonates with hiring executives in the current market. You need to promote your marketability to somebody who is scanning your document in perhaps twenty seconds or fewer.

Prepare an effective LinkedIn profile that will get you found by hiring executives and recruiters looking for experts like yourself. If you find the resume and career portfolio writing process daunting, as many entrepreneurs in your situation do, then engaging a career management consultant is a wise choice.

WHAT IF YOU'VE BEEN FIRED?

Let's face it—there is very little that is good about being fired. It has been said that job loss, and the ensuing loss of income, is one of life's biggest stressors. Furthermore, nobody could have predicted a global pandemic that would affect literally every aspect of our professional and personal lives. Many of my clients have been leading both the closure of their divisions and the shutdown of their own roles within them. Executives experiencing this type of crisis often believe that the best thing for them to do is to get right back in the saddle and go search for a new job. Instead of forcing yourself into a situation for which you are not fully prepared and to which you are not fully committed, pause for a moment and give yourself time to heal. Process what happened without the compounding pressure of engaging in a job search. Clear your head, read a dimestore novel, and spend time with your family—to the extent that the financial pressures bearing down on you are not dire. Take time to heal and evaluate your situation, then start hunting.

WHOM CAN YOU TRUST?

You'll find there are lots of resources available to move your career transition forward. But how do you know whom to trust throughout this process? Who has your best interests at heart?

Friends and Family

You may ask your spouse, your friend, or even your parent for advice. People in your close circle of trust will have your best interests at heart, but they are among the least objective about what will work for you. They know you well and have a good sense of what your strengths and salient characteristics are, but their own self-interest or personal interest in your well-being might interfere with your ability to find a position that satisfies all of your professional requirements.

Your Coworkers or Executive Manager

Among those who might offer you solid career advice are your professional peers or executive leaders to test your logic and help you move forward. However, know that as much as they have your best interests in mind, they also have agendas. They might compete with you, or they might ask you to take on more than your fair share. As you work your way up through the executive tiers of a company, you can pay attention to the needs and wishes and wants of your colleagues and superiors, but they might not give the best advice if they don't understand your specific aspirations, particularly if these fall outside your current company.

A Mentor

You are among the privileged if you can find and secure a mentor who can stand apart from you and provide you with rock-solid career advice. Finding a mentor can be challenging, but it can be extraordinarily rewarding as well if the mentor truly has a vested interest in your success. The best way to find a mentor is to identify the best-in-class for your industry or role. This presents a particular challenge as you will need to do some serious research to identify that person and then pitch your wish to be his or her protégé. A good mentor who fulfills the role successfully is an incomparable asset to your career advancement. This trusted guide will provide an insider's view of an industry or role while remaining objective and honest about your unique career pathway and agnostic about the company you ultimately join.

This person is likely to:

- have personally demonstrated executive excellence
- know a lot about the executive job function
- know a lot about the industry
- be noncompetitive, given that he/she sits several rungs above you on the traditional corporate ladder
- have your best interests in mind, although this person might not know you well enough to like you personally

To find your mentor in your executive job search, you should be willing to:

- **Look outside your field.** Often, you can get insight and objective opinions from someone not in your industry. This mentor may expand your thought processes about your career.
- **Collaborate on projects.** This is a great way to get to know potential mentors. You are both invested in a common goal. Working together can deepen your relationship and provide you with common interests.
- **Make your relationship reciprocal.** Your mentor will want to know how you are doing, what progress you are making, and what is working for you. Share your results. Offer insights and opinions (if asked) on your mentor's projects.
- **Determine when and how often you will meet.** Predetermining this information sets the expectation that you both will be professional and prepared to work. This is not a social meeting; you are both busy people. Your meetings with your mentor will vary in length and topic, depending on your needs. Prepare for your meetings and the ensuing discussion, which may include updates on your current projects, potential opportunities, and professional development strategy.

When requesting mentorship, promise that person you will not abuse the relationship by relying on them to offer you a specific executive job. That is not the role of this person in your career search; it is to support you with solid advice and insights available only to someone at that level.

As you develop your relationship, your interaction with your mentor may change. They may discover your opinion is a valuable resource, and you might have insights that can inform their growth. Remember, you both hope to share knowledge, insight, and opportunities.

A Trusted Board of Personal Directors

More broadly, you might want a team of people on whose opinions or advice you can rely. Calling on author, academic, and consultant Jim Collins' original idea for students of Stanford Business School, your personal board of directors is a team of individuals whom you have formally asked to give you knowledge and insights about yourself, even when the truth is uncomfortable. You can choose this team based on their level, experience in your industry, or their willingness to be unflinchingly honest with you.

Although you can have as many members on your personal board of directors as you wish, the core team should reflect at least these four types:

- **The Connector.** One who knows many people and can facilitate introductions.
- **The Challenger.** One who will not let you follow unsubstantiated lines of logic.
- **The Clarifier.** One who will ask you question after question to help you uncover hidden truths about yourself and your executive environment.
- **The Wise Elder.** One with senior status who serves as the typical mentor, listening to you and advising you.

A Recruiter

If you have worked with a recruiter to fill roles in your organization, you might find this person is a tremendous asset to your own executive career transition. The recruiter might seek someone just like you, or they might know somebody who is. Recruiters can be your best confidential advocates if they have identified you as a unique resource to pitch to their clients. Those who reach out to you likely have exclusivity on positions—ranging from director-level to CEO openings—that you would not otherwise learn about.

However, there are pitfalls: You have to trust the recruiter will keep under wraps your desire to leave your company, and the value of this relationship flows according to the money. Recruiters don't work for the job seeker; they work for the company that pays them. Candidates such as you are in the category of "talent" rather than "particular person I want to help." You can trust a recruiter to recommend you for positions, but expect little in the way of hands-on treatment from someone who has perhaps dozens of roles to fill and hundreds of candidates to review daily.

Know that spreading yourself thinly across a pool of recruiters dilutes your uniqueness; they can find you if they need you. If a recruiter calls, unprompted, to ask about your interest in a particular position, that's a conversation for which you should always make time (and, as a footnote, calls from "recruiters" hoping that you will pay them to find you a job are calls you should be fully skeptical of taking).

An Executive Career Coach and Resume Writer

A career coach is a professional dedicated to the career transition success of others. The career coach works directly for the executive and delivers world-class advice, coaching, and sometimes explicit consultation to individuals requiring a partner in the executive career transition process. Often, career coaches and resume writers have credentials from career management organizations validating training in the field, or they may have won major global awards for work in their respective fields. Executive career coaches and resume writers explore your career history, determine how those details match with your stated career goals, and translate what you have done into the language of the audience on whom you hope to make a glowing impression. You need to decide if you are ready to put in the work required to make your career transition successful. It involves soul-searching, a willingness to reach out to new people, readiness to accept a great deal of direction, and a drive to be the best in your position and your field.

Your executive career coach and resume writer can be your best advocate throughout your career transition. This professional is always on your side, helping you to develop clarity for your:

- target executive title
- target industry
- target company
- messaging and storytelling
- career portfolio (e.g., your executive resume and cover letter)
- social media presence, including but not limited to LinkedIn profile development

PART 2

CRAFT

— 4 —

STOP WRITING YOUR RESUME

THERE IS NO EASY PATH TO GROWTH

SOME SAY THERE IS NO ROYAL ROAD TO LEARNING. In the same way, there is no royal road to executive job search success. Regardless of who you are, what your role is, and what your accomplishments have been over the last decade or more, your job search will be hard. Few individual mechanisms will guarantee that you save time in the task ahead.

Now, don't get me wrong, I truly wish that a well-prepared executive resume, targeted and replete with grand accomplishments, would solve all the job-search obstacles that executives face. Usually, however, the task is much more complex. The soul-searching that businesspeople like you must go through to establish a direction that makes sense, tap into a productive network, build a marketing program, and execute a successful job search takes time and a healthy dose of hard work.

If you are looking for a quick fix, you are not likely to find one. If somebody promises you a low-cost quick fix, dig a little deeper both inside yourself and inside what you are being offered to determine if such a panacea is possible. Throughout the next few chapters, we'll take a hard look at the most difficult aspects of the process and help you design a path to resolving the biggest questions first.

YOUR SEARCH DOES NOT START WITH YOUR RESUME

Yes, the title says it all. Stop writing your executive resume right now. Put down your pencil, turn off your computer, and stop capturing your voice into your smartphone. This probably goes against everything you've been taught about job hunting, but it is true. If the first thing you do in your executive career search is write your resume, you are bound to lengthen your task—possibly from a few months to years—if not fail altogether. Save time, be strategic, and avoid falling prey to the most unfortunate myth about job hunting with this one strategic tip.

The five top pitfalls of starting a job search by writing your resume are clear:

1. You have not yet identified the industry within which you want to work.

2. You have not yet selected a job level, whether it is individual contributor, manager, director, vice president, COO, or CEO.

3. You do not know how to temper your entrepreneurial roots to fit into a thriving organization.

4. You do not know which jobs you should apply for, but you think you will find them on job boards.

5. You believe you can pull out, capture, and write about exactly what a future hiring executive needs to know about you, on your own.

But I Need a Resume, Right Now!

You need a resume, right? Yes, correct, and soon. To get to that point, you might ignore the foregoing and hammer out a resume yourself, even though you don't have full answers to these questions. What could that document possibly say? In my experience, these "resumes" are regurgitation of whatever the human resources team thinks your job descriptions have been.

Resume writers, especially those working exclusively with executive-level job seekers, see the process completely differently. We want to know what your job descriptions were, but more than that, we want to know how well you did your job plus what you want to do next. Before we commit anything to paper, we take a step back and evaluate these three important questions:

1. What do you want to do next?

2. Does your future goal look like your recent career history?

3. Does your future goal look like your distant career history?

If you do not know the answer to any of these questions, you are not ready to write your resume. In fact, a smart executive resume writer will tell you that you are probably about five to eight weeks away from being ready. Those unusual details become the very reasons your resume will be selected from the heap on the hiring team's desk, and we want to be sure that we understand your entire self-presentation, not just the part of you that needs this done faster than fast without the right strategy behind it. You will find that hiring an expert executive resume writer has these benefits—and more. I would encourage you not to skimp on this important investment any more than I would advise that your company hire the cheapest marketing manager or operations leader you can find (or worse, hire nobody at all).

Put Your Resume Aside and Start Thinking Strategically

I know you wanted to get started right away, now that you have decided it is time to switch careers. But, again, starting with your resume is a poor strategy. Instead, take some time to focus on the following stages:

1. Pick an industry. You will not fit into every industry, but you will fit squarely into one or two.

2. Select the right job level for you, knowing that in some cases, the authority of a given title will vary by industry, company, and company size.

3. If you have most recently been an entrepreneur, start to think about your role as an executive leader rather than a start-up type. Keep the hunger; lose the lone cowboy approach.

4. Select a category of jobs, then use LinkedIn, your existing network, and strategic networking techniques to meet the right decision makers—or those who can effectively introduce you to the people you need to meet.

5. Hire an executive career coach and resume writer. If you hit a wall and don't have a good sense of what your career goals should be, an executive career coach and resume writer can walk you through a highly customized process that helps

you figure this out. You will explore a variety of career paths and talk to the right people who can inform your career search.

While you evaluate your options in a fairly safe environment and feed that information back into your strategy, you can then start to think about the shape of your executive resume. I am certain that you will see the result of your work and a natural progression that funnels into the writing process. You will also see that you have tremendous work yet to do, so you will want to stick with the plan your executive career coach and resume writer have established for you and let them walk the path with you to your success.

This process might go against what you believe is conventional wisdom; however, once you have completed these steps, you will see an immediate shift in the pace of your search—all because you stopped writing and started strategizing.

— 5 —

STRATEGY FOR SUCCESS

FOCUS YOUR RESEARCH

If you have been in the executive job search market for a while, you might wonder what it takes to get noticed and hired by the right company. In fact, the longer you search, the more frustrated you become. One reason you might fail to earn recognition in the marketplace is that you cannot articulate what you want to do and in which industry you want to do it. The following simple plan will help focus your strategy to make you the most memorable candidate on the list.

Step 1: Figure Out What You Want to Do

On the face of it, this is obvious. You want an executive job, probably related to your prior experience. Yes, you might be at the point where any post looks good, as long as it is not what you are doing now (or delivers a reliable paycheck). But the answer will be much more complicated than that. Remember, you need to be realistic about your goals and understand that neither industries nor companies will bend to your wants and needs until you prove your value to them.

Your Plan: Do some free writing or some unfettered speculation about the solutions you want to contribute.

1. Create an "ideal job" description of the job you want. Describe the job title, type of company, location, responsibilities, compensation/benefits, and so on.

2. Identify which of your skills are most marketable to a prospective employer. Make a list of your skills: customer service, sales, technology, communication, etc. Clarifying your skills will not only help in your job search but will also help you identify which skills, training, education, and experience to emphasize on your resume.

3. Answer these questions: What am I good at? What am I not so good at? What do I like doing? What skills do I need to update to stay current?

Know What You Do Not Want in a Job

Rather than start with what you want in a future executive position, a different tactic is to identify all the functions you definitely don't want in a role. Thus, your job search will exclude all the elements of a job you do not want to have.

In this employment economy, there is no be-all, know-all, do-all executive. While you need to be flexible about the work you take on, expanding your role once you are in a position, you will not be interviewed, much less selected for hire, if your unique selling point is that you can do anything.

Think of the Venn diagram we all learned in junior high school math: It has three or four overlapping circles that identify sets of elements. Some elements are in all sets, and some are in just one. Think about your potential jobs as these overlapping circles. Are the positions you have chosen very much alike? If so, your circles overlap significantly. If they do not overlap, then you have a complex process of elimination before you. You need to identify exactly what you do not want in a position, those deal-killing job functions that fit into only one of the circles. These roles are ones you can eliminate.

Now look at the positions you have left. Are these ideal for you? Do they overlap? By how much? The less they overlap, the more pruning you have to do to home in on your perfect role. Determine which of the remaining job characteristics, perhaps the ones that fall into two job types, you can cut from your short list. By this point, you should have a tightly nested or overlapping set of circles representing a sharply focused set of job titles.

With this renewed focus, which eliminated the roles you would never assume, you can now craft an executive job search that positions you 100 percent on target. The benefits of this approach are many, and when you market yourself so compellingly for the perfect job in the ideal company, hiring teams cannot help but recognize the solution to their problems in your candidacy.

Step 2: Identify the Right Industry

Your job function may have correlates across multiple industries, so you might believe you can fit in almost anywhere. This could be true, but "I can do anything—put me in anywhere and I'll succeed!" is a hard sell and nearly impossible to communicate in a properly constructed resume or during an interview. Your resume needs to target your assets relative to a particular industry, company, and, ultimately, position or category of positions. Your interview should convey your experience so that the hiring executive sees you are the solution to their problems. Thus, you need to determine which industry or sub-industry you will best fit into, and in which you will feel most rewarded.

Your Plan: Look at your current industry broadly to evaluate whether you still fit into it. Then determine whether additional industries might be more compelling to you.

1. Does your current industry provide sufficient interest for you to continue in it?
2. Are you finding the right challenges on a broad level?
3. Are there interesting problems that you can solve?
4. Are your ethics aligned with the success of your industry?
5. Do you believe that you can contribute over the long term to the success of your industry?

6. Have you explored other industries that might capture your interest? If so, you need to figure out what is interesting about them.

Read voraciously. Explore industry resources, regional business journals, company websites, and public relations pieces to inform your knowledge of the industry. You'll learn more about the state of the employment economy by learning which companies are getting funded or are growing by reading about their goals and strategies than you will by reading their job postings. As you build out your network to include people in those industries, you'll get an insider's view of the way the industry works.

Step 3: Target the Right Companies

Now that you have a good sense of the industry landscape, it is time to narrow down your list of company targets. Make a list of the companies on which you want to focus. These companies should hire for the work you want to do, in the industry in which you want to do it.

Your Plan: Look across your target industry, then narrow your set of company targets.

1. Start by evaluating the market in which you want to work and live. Limit your searches to this geography to start.

2. Use Indeed.com, LinkedIn.com, and the many specialty job boards just to get a sense of who is hiring for what positions, but DO NOT apply online for these positions (yet).

3. Rather than apply for ten jobs per week online, reach out to a few key people per week. These people should work in the companies you've targeted or know people who do. Make appointments with them for informational interviews.

4. Use local business journals and newspapers as resources to learn about regional companies in your industry, particularly if they are receiving funding or moving to larger space—both indicate corporate growth and, potentially, intent to hire new personnel.

5. Read company blogs to learn whether you are interested in their missions, goals, activities, products, and more.

6. Do not let recruiters coax you into applying for positions in your *target* company through them. Present yourself to the right companies first, before you let recruiters show you with a 25–30 percent markup to your salary. Note: This rule only applies to your top-10 company list at the start of your job search. Recruiters can be significant assets to your job search, especially if they present to you roles that are otherwise part of the "hidden" job market.

Take Note

- Do not be discouraged if a particular company is not posting the job you want to do on its career site. Your strategies need to be focused and include building your network of people inside or related to those companies.

- Do not just focus on large companies in your job search. Small and mid-size companies—including start-ups—are a significant source of new job opportunities. Do not discount a company just on its size; think about its growth potential or life cycle stage.

Step 4: Start Looking at the Right Positions

Congratulations! You've spent a great deal of time and effort learning about the work you find fulfilling and the industry in which you want to do it, compiling a list of jobs that make sense for you. Now you need to get very specific so you can start applying for the ideal positions.

Your Plan: For this phase of your job search, you need to develop, at minimum, a three-point strategy.

1. Learn more about the specific role you want to play by learning the needs of the companies you have targeted.

Start by looking at the blogs, public relations efforts, and news reports of the companies you have targeted. Learn about their pain points and develop a narrative about your own history that directly explains how you can serve companies to improve their situations. For example, if you are a CFO and your target company is expanding, you might talk about the ways you can improve daily cash flow to support rapid growth. If you are a real estate analyst, you might talk about your experience in site selection. If you are a vice president of sales and marketing, you might speak to a company's need to steadily increase business so that the infrastructure can manage the growth well.

Now identify the specific opportunities within those companies through which you can address those needs, perhaps on company websites or in one of the major job engines. Do not neglect to review the company's Facebook page, LinkedIn company profile, Instagram, Snapchat, or even its Craigslist listings. Keep a record of what you learn that you can follow and review.

2. Speak more deeply and broadly to your network about available positions.
You likely know someone, or know someone who knows someone, at your target company. If not, go back to LinkedIn and build the relationships that will get you closer to the hiring executive. We discuss this process further in chapters 10 and 11. Once you have these key connections, talk to the hiring executive directly if you can. People hire people, so the relationships you build early on will support your application for the roles you want in the future.

3. Develop a career portfolio that speaks to these positions directly, compelling your audience to understand the value you will deliver to them.
Now you can start building your resume and cover letter. Combined with your LinkedIn profile, these should speak directly to the roles you are pitching for. Generally, your executive resume should target a category of positions within a particular industry so that tweaking it for each position applied is straightforward. Know that a resume not targeted to a role in a particular industry will not get you the interviews you want; moreover, a resume targeted to a different role or different industry will not compel a hiring executive to reach out to you, either. In chapters 6 to 9 we focus on preparing an outstanding resume and cover letter.

You should now have a solid understanding of the positions right for you *and* likely to be available, a great network to help you get an insider's connection to the hiring executive, and an executive career portfolio that addresses your career history which considers a future hiring executive's needs.

Step 5: Apply for the Subset of Positions That Match Your Goals, Your Needs, and Company Demands

There are three key ways to apply for an executive position that's right for you: directly on a company's career website or job board; through recruiters; and, most effectively, networking. Each of these strategies can be effective if you use them the right way.

Your plan: Explore career websites and job boards, recruiter needs, and your network's capability to develop an executive job application strategy.

1. Apply online for executive jobs: 5 percent of your job search effort.
Know that using job boards and career sites is the *least* effective job search strategy, particularly for senior executives, although it is one of the easiest. You should spend only 5 percent of your job search effort using this method.

To make this strategy work for you while not eating into the time you should be spending on more effective techniques, take advantage of alerts. Google alerts are easy to set up, as are alerts from Indeed.com and some of the other major job boards; LinkedIn also has a great alert system.

First, develop a Boolean query (a search combining keywords with AND, NOT, and OR) that returns the results you are seeking. You can use the query in all of your alerts so you don't miss a critical opportunity. Note that not all systems use strict Boolean techniques, so you might need to test the minus sign or NOT to eliminate undesirable results. You might need to test your queries multiple times to make sure they are returning the results you want. The alerts will run in the background and be emailed to you on the schedule you determine; you can review the results of your job search quickly and easily without having to run individual queries every day. Considering that job boards and online applications are the least effective use of your energies, alerts simplify the process for you.

Note: Some companies with large online application systems will require applicants at every level to apply through their online application systems, regardless of their networking strategies. Make sure that you follow the policies of each company that you are targeting.

2. Engage with recruiters: 20 percent of your job search effort.
Strictly speaking, you do not work with recruiters; recruiters work with the companies that hire them to fill key positions. The "talent," in this case, you, the applicant, is almost tangential to the process, which is dictated by the flow of dollars.

Roughly speaking, from a cash flow perspective, the recruiting process looks like this:

1. The company uses a recruiter, either contract or contingent (more on that below), to find an ideal pool of candidates.

2. The company evaluates these career portfolios and chooses several to interview. The company might also interview candidates whom they source internally or who apply outside of the recruiting process.

3. The career portfolios do not become valuable as individuals until they bring the candidates in for interviews with the executive hiring team.

4. The company hires a candidate offered by the recruiter or sourced by some other means.

5. The selected candidate chooses, or not, to accept the position. If a recruiter presented the successful candidate, the recruiting agency receives a finder's commission of as much as 30 percent of the candidate's first year's salary.

When you are presented by a recruiter to a company, you automatically come with a fairly expensive price tag—commissions can range from 10–30 percent of your first year's salary—perhaps $30,000 or more. Thus, hiring through a recruiter is an exceptionally expensive proposition, and some companies categorically refuse to follow this path.

Therefore, you need to do two things. First, you need to apply to your target list. If you present yourself first, regardless of whether a recruiter presents you later, you do not come with a price tag. Know your target list and apply before the recruiter does.

Second, know the status of the recruiter who presents you to a company. Recruiters are "contingent" or "contract." Contingent recruiters are not in formal relationships with companies, meaning they are sourcing candidates in competition with other similar contingency recruiters. Contract recruiters will get paid regardless of whether they source and place for a particular position, although their reputations demand results of the highest quality. Know the relationship a recruiter has with a company, and you will know more about the flow of dollars and your position as a candidate in that flow. Never let a recruiter present you to a company without your express permission—you might not want a recruiter to present you to a company on your target list.

The one instance in which you absolutely should let a recruiter present you is when they have insider knowledge of a confidential search that you would never learn about through other means. This situation is ideal for you and the recruiter, and you both have a real stake in the outcome.

3. **Network into the right role before it becomes available: 75 percent of your job search effort.**

Your networking efforts should focus on developing relationships early in your executive job search so you are uniquely top of mind when positions become available. This is a time-consuming process and not one that will bear fruit early on. But it is highly effective as a job search strategy in the long term if you do it consistently and correctly.

To network effectively, you need to listen, learn, and communicate so your audience believes that the conversation is a two-way street. Build relationships while you are still in your current role, while you are in job-search mode, and when you have secured your next position. Keep contacts warm throughout your career, and you can capitalize on them when you need to. We'll talk more about networking in chapter 10.

LOOKING FOR WORK IS NOW YOUR FULL-TIME JOB

Would You Hire Yourself during Your Job Search?

If you're unemployed, looking for work should now be your full-time job. Although your effort to look for work in this tough economy isn't something you can put on a resume, your job search has to be your prime focus, and that means up to forty hours per week.

Does a forty-hour weekly investment seem too much? Think about it this way. If you worked for a company and didn't spend every valuable moment doing something productive, you'd be fired. If you hired someone else to find you a job and that person failed, you would fire them too. So, if you're not looking for work for a standard number of hours each week, fire that character and take on a new, successful job-searching persona.

If You Worked Only Twenty-Two Minutes per Week, You'd Be Fired

Some time ago, a major research institution reported on the way unemployed people use their time instead of searching for work. It turns out people sleep more, work on their houses more, and attend to their medical care. But they don't spend a great deal of time looking for work. Surprisingly, they spend only 1 percent of their time in job search mode. If a typical workweek is about thirty-seven hours, the average unemployed person is spending twenty-two minutes per week looking for work.

Each Activity Should Have a Purpose

Every hour, every minute you spend on some other activity during work hours is unrecoverable time lost that you could be using productively looking for a job.

- **Join a job club.** There are in-person job clubs, virtual job clubs, formal and informal job clubs—and all are designed to help you look for work.
- **Get training.** You've got the time, so go take a class in something you can talk about in your next interview. It also fills that gap on the resume since your last position.
- **Shadow someone in a new industry or position for a day.** Learn what they do. Ask questions. Pay attention. This might be your job target.
- **Network with people you know—and people you don't.** Expand your circle. Become visible.
- **Apply intelligently for jobs.** Your resume is one key to your success. Tweak it for those choice positions.

Don't just "do" something. Everything you do in your job search should have a purpose. If you don't have a strategy and have no idea what the best use of your time is while you are looking for work, invest in guidance from a career coach.

BE EFFICIENT

As you think about your career search and define your strategy, these few simple processes can help you wisely manage the time you spend on your job hunt.

Clean Your Desk

They say that a cluttered desk is a sign of a creative mind, but it's also a sign that you've gotten off track with your plan. Take fifteen minutes every morning to go through an old stack of papers; file those bills, and collate all those business cards you've collected over the years.

Simple strategy for today:

Convert those business cards to LinkedIn connections. Invite each of those new contacts to join your online network, and make sure you invite them with a short note that reminds them of how you met.

Make a List of the Contacts You've Been Meaning to Call

Get your networking strategy off the ground by determining whom you need to reach. Networking—online or in real life—is now the number-one method of finding a job. For you to use this critical network effectively, you'll need to record each contact, what they said, and when you plan to reach them again.

Simple strategy for today:

Build a networking spreadsheet. Label the columns with name, dates, subject, industry, and anything else you find relevant to your job search. Keep this record of your contacts up to date, and you'll always have a handy reference to your networking strategy.

Answer a LinkedIn Question

Remind your LinkedIn contacts that you're still in the game and that you truly are an expert in your field. Pick a question or two and deliver great resources. You'll prove yourself to be an online expert and likely gain some new connections for your network (see #2 above).

Simple strategy for today:

It takes a lot of effort to use online resources effectively without getting distracted by all of the possibilities the web has to offer. Commit to answering one or two questions, then walk away from your computer. Don't spin your wheels trying to find a job online when you could call a contact or go to a networking group in real time or face-to-face.

Read a Book on Career Search Strategy

My weekly trips to the bookstore reveal that there are simply dozens of career strategy books. Clear your mind and soak up valuable information at the same time (not to mention a great cup of coffee). Sit down for an hour and learn something new. Can't make it to the bookstore? Try your public library's e-book section and read for free.

Simple strategy for today:

The next time you're on LinkedIn, ask this question of your network: What is the best book you've read on improving your career search strategy? You'll get some amazing advice, and, again, effortlessly build your connection base.

Do Whatever It Was You Were Planning to Do for Your Career Search but Got Sidetracked

We all get sidetracked. It's human nature to be attracted to the next best thing. I know you've had something in your head you've been meaning to do that you simply keep forgetting to do. Set a time and a date to do this one thing and commit to getting it done.

Simple strategy for today:

Write down this one thing you have been meaning to do. Someone once said that a goal is only a wish until you write it down—make this one thing an actual task with deadlines and boundaries. Put this goal on an index card and tape it above your desk. When you finish, hang up another index card with another goal. You'll be amazed at how much you can complete and how far your own personal career search strategy will take you.

— 6 —

PREPARE AN OUTSTANDING RESUME

WHY BUILD A RESUME?

Before we get started, take thirty seconds to brainstorm the answer to this question: what is a resume for?

Perhaps you came up with one or two of the following answers:

- To demonstrate your skills.
- To give a hiring manager a reason to pay you some attention.
- To encourage a recruiter to put you in his database of potential candidates.
- To show what an outstanding employee you are.
- To demonstrate your achievements.
- To list your education and certifications.
- The list goes on, and I'm sure you had a few ideas of your own.

But they're wrong.

The goal of a resume is TO GET YOU THE INTERVIEW. That's it. There are a million resume self-improvement sound bites out there, some useful, most useless. But these are simply techniques for grabbing the brass ring.

Remember, the only point of your resume is to market yourself in the best way possible to get the interview. From there, it's all about what you say, how you present yourself, and how you negotiate on your own behalf.

WHY DOES YOUR RESUME DRIVE YOUR INTERVIEW? (IT IS NOT WHAT YOU THINK)

You're now thinking that the relationship between your resume and your interview is obvious. I've just said that your resume gets you the interview, right? Certainly, an expertly prepared resume that a hiring leader cannot ignore will generate the interview you need. However, in every well-conceived job search strategy, your interview is actually a reflection of your resume, not the reverse.

Let us assume that you have set up your dream interview. In your excitement, you prepare in every way you think possible:

- You wear the right suit.

- You read the right books on how to answer questions on your weaknesses and other tricky points.

- You learn something about the CEO's latest initiatives so you can hold a savvy conversation.

The one thing you do not do is brush up on yourself. You have no idea how to talk about your career experiences and accomplishments. In fact, the first time you put your stories into words is at the request of the interviewer to tell something about your expertise. Because you have not prepared for the task, you fail. You are practicing when you should be performing.

You can avoid this major interview pitfall by having an expert resume writer prepare your resume. With their input, you're more likely to increase the number of interviews you receive and improve your level of success throughout the interview process.

Let us examine why. When you choose your resume writer, you will have sought a professional who will give you uninterrupted one-on-one attention. He or she will draw you through extensive questions and answers to elicit the best of your experience and accomplishments. This might be the first time you ever have verbalized your expertise, so you can feel free to take your time to explore and elaborate on your talents, history, skills, and specific achievements. Through this process, you'll have the privilege of telling yourself the story first, then seeing a distillation of your reports in a well-crafted, professionally written executive resume.

Now let us reimagine your interview. When the interviewing executive asks you to relate some specific expertise, you can do so confidently. At this point, you are retelling a story that you've told yourself, had told to you, and reviewed extensively. You will be eminently ready to walk your interviewer through your career history—more so because you have had your resume professionally prepared.

CRAFTING THE BEST RESUME FOR YOU AND YOUR UNIQUE JOB SEARCH

The best resume you can write—or that a resume writing professional can write for you—is

- unique to your specific job search
- targeted to the positions you are trying to obtain
- authentically reflective of your specific career history and your personal brand.

There are hundreds of articles on resume personal branding. There are perhaps thousands of articles on resume accomplishment statements. However, strictly speaking, using accomplishments in your bullets alone won't convert your history into your unique branding, or make your career history into the best resume it can be.

You could research resume examples written for anonymous other members of your industry (or look at a friend's) and copy the bullets word for word. You could also use resume writing systems that you buy on the internet, which are simply lists of bullets that you can use in your resume. And there are the professional resume writers who won't even talk to you before embarking on the tricky process of writing a resume that best suits your job search.

These seemingly simple systems don't work. They do not capture your authenticity. If you want to be authentic in your job search and to find the best fit for your specific job search needs, you need to think about your resume as an organic document that is borne of your particular personal history. Even if you worked in a factory, or if you ran one, you are not a factory yourself. There's no such thing as data-in, data-out in a resume writing process that gets you interviews. It's much more thoughtful and careful than that.

The following are the minimum steps I follow to write the best resume that fits your specific job search needs.

1. I learn about what makes you special.

2. I learn about what makes you unique.

3. I ask you about every aspect of your job, in the context of your position, role, and industry.

4. I translate where you have been in your career to where you want to go, in the language of and according to the expectations of your audience.

When I start a resume writing project, I start with a blank screen. Yes, this process is tougher than using a resume template, but it's much more authentic. I start from scratch because I make sure that each client receives 100 percent unique content that is 100 percent about his or her specific career history, branding, and personal excellence. You deserve no less than this attention and devotion to the most important subject of the day: You.

Of course, if you're captivated by the idea of writing down your entire career history, this is not a wasted exercise. I call it "building the ten-page resume," and I believe every executive has to do this at some point in their career. If you worked with me, I would have you do a more organized version of this, and it would be a comprehensive repository of everything you've ever accomplished in your entire life. Not all of this content would find a home in the resume you're building today, but it would serve as the well from which we draw as we work together.

SHOW PRIDE AND HUMILITY IN YOUR RESUME

I am constantly amazed at the level of success of the executive job seekers with whom I work daily. They run companies. They drive sales. They lead international teams. They are among the smartest I have met regarding technology. They are rightfully proud of what they have done. Yet, they are among the humblest people I have ever met. By infusing their executive resumes with this pride and humility, they prove they are true leaders in their industries without coming across as boastful and overblown.

Here are three statements I hear all the time from my clients. Develop these into compelling accomplishment stories, showing both pride in your leadership and the knowledge that you are only as good as the amazing team you develop and lead into the fray:

1. **"It was my talented team who really did it; we all worked together."** Executive leaders rarely deliver at the individual contributor level. They understand, however, that the team cannot succeed without their unifying leadership. Therefore, rather than going on about their individual tactical role, they rightfully focus on how they guided the team to larger goals.

2. **"I have an uncanny ability to hire the right people and place them throughout the company where they can do the most good."** By showing insight into which people are right for your organization, you achieve two goals. You show you are wise to the larger industry, and you demonstrate that you can read people very well. Include details in your executive resume about your hiring strategy and the way you assess future team members.

3. **"I always hire people who are smarter than I am."** This is my favorite. Nobody likes to work for a paranoid organization, and when an executive leader states outright that they will hire team members with particular expertise or savvy that they don't have, it shows a healthy mix of fearlessness and pride.

In short, don't be afraid to recognize that you are not always the smartest guy in the room. It's a big leap to embrace this mindset, especially when, in your early career, you were always hungry for the next win. Now, as a wiser, more tempered executive leader, if you're smart, your executive resume will show that much of the credit also goes to a rock star team. In doing so, your ability to guide a group to a successful outcome shows you honor your company and every team member. Communicating your talents and value with humility and pride will win the attention of like-minded hiring leaders.

Leveling vs Bragging

Bragging is unpleasant. Nobody wants to do it, and nobody wants to hear it. Bragging is when you talk about yourself in a way that is overinflated and has no substance. And unsubstantiated bragging on your resume is highly transparent.

But that's not you. You're an executive, and you have a high-powered career. Talk about your accomplishments so your audience understands that what you offer is substantive and valuable. That's called leveling. Describe exactly what happened, with the right metrics to corroborate your expertise, without telling them whether they should like what you've done or believe the success is relevant to their organization. Give your audience the facts of the case and your career history without boasting and drive home the point that you bring something unusual and highly valuable to a future executive team.

The Dunning-Kruger Effect

When a company's leadership fails, it's easy for us on the outside to point out what we believe would have been a better corporate choice. I have no hard breakdown of the data on what executives think as they look backward to review their strategies, but there's probably a decent split—some feel they made the right choice, regardless of the outcome, and some truly regret their decisions.

As you look at your career, maybe you don't know what to think about specific choices you made for your organization. It's been reported that very bright people are more anxious about their performance—you might fall into this category.

More troubling is the reverse, called the Dunning-Kruger effect. This psychological phenomenon represents a false sense of security in the rightness and power of one's ability despite proof to the contrary. This proof might appear in the form of objectively bad business decisions or subjectively poor performance as measured against that of peers. Simply stated, smart people worry about doing better; those who perform at a lower level are cognitively biased against recognizing their capability.

How do you see your work history? Are you proud of every decision you've made? Do you wish you had done better? On the flip side, does your career feel perfect? Take a few seconds to digest these questions as you prepare for the next phase in your career.

RESUME VERSUS JOB APPLICATION: WHAT'S THE DIFFERENCE? AND WHY DOES IT MATTER?

Many companies require you to fill out a job application even though a resume is already in the hands of the hiring manager. While this may seem unnecessary repetition on your part, there are several reasons that companies want both the resume and the job application, which benefit the candidate and the hiring company. But if the information you provide on these two important career documents does not match, proceed at the peril of your interview and possibly your career.

Your Resume

Think of your resume as advertising on your background. It provides the branding that you want to bring to your interview, makes you shine during the interview process, and details the assets you bring to a future employer.

A resume provides a job candidate with an organized and structured method to present work experiences and achievements, educational background, membership in professional organizations and pertinent community involvement. Include any continuing education courses to the resume, especially if they align with the prospective company's interests.

Your Job Application

The job application offers a company a legal document that states all information provided is true and allows the interviewer to look further into your background. Well-designed employment applications often will ask for more complete details about why a person left a position or compensation history.

Applications are part of your official record with a company. Making sure that your resume and application information align is important. An interviewer will catch discrepancies even if done in error. Both the resume and job application need to be complete and honest. Lying on either is an issue, especially since the job application is a legal document. Most applications have wording that states that all information provided is true, complete and accurate.

Does Your Resume Match Your Job Application?

A mismatch between your resume and job search could be cause for immediate rejection by a target company (or termination, if you're already employed). Don't risk it. The more honest you are about your history, the more authentic your career story is. If you are having trouble telling your history due to complexities in your timeline (terminations, job-hopping, and so on), a career coach and resume writer can help you message that story appropriately. If you haven't quite finished your degree or never attended university, your resume writer can work with the education you do have to promote you effectively. In other words, trust that your resume writer has faced complexities such as these—and more—and will be comfortable designing a strategy to highlight your expertise and the benefits of hiring you over the potential issues your career history might present.

RESUME SECTIONS THAT MATTER TO HIRING EXECUTIVES

Have you ever wondered what parts of your executive resume really matter to the hiring team? The key pieces might not be what you think.

Your Name

Always put your name at the top of your resume. Double-check to ensure that your name is spelled properly. If you use your middle name or initial, ensure that this is included and spelled correctly as well.

Your name might be the most important piece of identifying information, but it might be getting in your way as you apply for jobs.

Your Name Is Common

When you look in the phone book for your name, are there a dozen other John Smiths before and after your own John Smith? You are unique among your colleagues, company, and industry, but your name might be so common that a quick search of LinkedIn does not immediately bring your profile to the top of the list. Thus, new networking contacts do not know how to learn anything about you via LinkedIn or other social media profiles.

The Quick Fix:

Start using your middle name or middle initial to differentiate yourself.

Some Unsavory Character Has Your Name, Too

Does a quick search of your name bring up a mug shot that is not yours? Do people believe that the mug shot or court case record might be yours, just because you have the same name as someone with less integrity than you? Certainly, a purported criminal or civil case history, the records for which are all available online, can interfere with your ability to get proper attention from hiring executives if the mix-up between names is easy to make.

The Quick Fix:

Use your first initial, middle initial and/or middle name, and last name, plus your credentials, in every instance of social media, across all uses and profiles on the internet. Also use this name configuration on your resume, business cards, phone messages, and voice mail. Do not use it on job applications, as you will need to use your full legal name for those documents.

Your Name Is Unusual

You might know that your name is perfectly normal, but if you suspect that the words or syllables of your name have an unintended or humorous meaning to them, you might not be receiving interview offers because of this subtlety.

The Quick Fix:

If your name provokes an inadvertent response, perhaps using only part of your hyphenated name, adding your middle name or initial, or using your first and middle initial plus last name only will help your audience focus on your expertise.

Your Name Is MISSING

If your resume starts with the word "Resume" on the first line, then this quick fix is for you. Applicant tracking systems require you to upload your resume online for job postings. If the word "Resume" is at the top of your document, the same word will populate the name field or fields of the system. Thus, to the company to which you are applying, your name will be Resume—just like the rest of those whose resumes did not start with their names and addresses.

The Quick Fix:

Take the word "Resume" off your resume—even if you never plan to upload your resume online. Using that as a heading is poor practice regardless.

Your Current Contact Information

Below your name, include your address, city, state, and zip code or, in some cases, your city and state only. Then include ONE phone number (mobile is usually best) and your current email address. You are welcome to include your full mailing address, although often your city, state, and ZIP code will be sufficient—you are not likely to receive snail mail in response to your resume in any case, but showing that you are in a specific geography could influence a hiring team not ready to pay for relocation.

Looking for work in your own region is difficult, but it is somewhat more complicated to succeed in a job search when you are looking to move to a new location. You might not have the time to go on cross-country treks for interviews, and you could be excluded from the running because you're not a "local" candidate. Let's look at some important strategies to improve your odds of getting interviews and job offers for executive jobs outside of your region.

Targeting Only Local Executive Positions

Your address places you in a specific location. If you are searching for a new executive role in your region, hiring leaders are likely to believe you have some flexibility around interviews and start dates. In most cases, an interview day will not require the expenses and frustrations of overnight travel. So, if you are applying for a local role, your local address could improve your chances of being selected for an interview based solely on the convenience factor, all else being equal among you and the other candidates.

Targeting the Right Openings Regardless of Their Location

If your address shows you're applying from a distance of hundreds or even thousands of miles, the hiring leader might exclude you based on the complexity of bringing you in and, ultimately, requiring a move across the country.

Therefore, you might include only your name, phone number, and professional email on your resume. This practice has become much more standard. Unlike decades past, your hiring executive is more likely to call your mobile phone or email you than send you a letter via the US Postal Service. For convenience, many people keep their longstanding mobile numbers no matter where they move. We have all encountered executives whose mobile phone area codes do not match their locations, and this practice raises few red flags.

Targeting Your Search on a Specific Region

If you are targeting a specific location across the state or country, you can set up a local address. Consider the following strategies:

- Secure a local street address in the city or region that you are targeting. The simplest method of doing this is to use a mailbox service with a street address in the new city.

- If you want to be upfront about your move, include the words "Relocating to" with a temporary local address.

- Get a telephone number with a local area code. Many inexpensive or free phone redirect services enable you to have a telephone number with a local area code that redirects to your existing home or mobile phone number.

Your Resume's Address: The Bottom Line

Your location matters in your job search for several key reasons, all of them financial. On the one hand, your hiring executive might want to interview all candidates within a certain period, which could make bringing candidates in from other regions difficult. On the other, the costs of moving a family across the country plus temporary housing, meals, and the search for a new home—called a relocation package—can be thousands of additional dollars added to the expenses of hiring a new executive.

Give Your Career History a Title

Never use the word "Resume" as a heading to your resume, as an application tracking system or online job application tool very well might interpret this to mean that your name is "Resume."

Instead, below your contact information, include the title of the position you currently have, the one you are seeking, or a general description of the type of role you are approaching if you have not formally held this title before. I have often joked that including this one line ensures the intern who opens the mail knows to whom he should give your resume, but the truth is that the title frames the document and primes the reader. The context you provide here gives the reader a sense of what is to come in the document and enables them to interpret your content the way you want them to.

Your Professional Branding Statement

A recent resume client of mine joked—wistfully—that she used to simply copy her job descriptions into her resume, and that was enough to secure her the interviews she wanted. Times have changed. Job descriptions are by their very nature generic. To make your resume compelling, you must describe the ways in which you are unique, specific, and ideal for the role, company, culture, and industry.

Thus, following the title to your career history, include a brief statement about your professional branding. Describe the characteristics of your professional persona that make you incomparable and valuable. In a concise self-evaluation, you will succinctly identify the ways you are uniquely qualified to exceed every single one of a hiring manager's expectations and solve all of the hiring team's problems. It has to demonstrate in about the length of time it takes to read this sentence exactly why you, and only you, are the right person to jump into the position today and take it to new levels beyond which the ordinary candidate could not possibly go. Even though this section lands first on the top of the page, and it usually is the first part of the resume your reader will digest, as the frame for your entire resume, it's likely to be the last thing you write.

Special note: Resumes used to be headed with the classic objective statement. Usually, this statement was dull and self-centered. For example, "I want to join a company that does great work and where I can grow as an amazing employee." I'm sure that's you, and I'm sure it's every job seeker—it's not a statement central to who you are as an employee, leader, or industry expert. Thus, heed this: Do not under any circumstances include an objective statement. This selfish, old-school "I want" will only serve to irritate your reader who, at this moment, truly does not care what you want. Instead, your branding statement will help them to want to know more about you (and, later, whatever it is that you do want).

Resume Storytelling in Three Easy Steps

As you start compiling your history, be aware of the biggest mistake you can make—describing your jobs one by one. You'll bore your audience, and they won't read beyond the first line or two of each position you've held. Change your strategy and minimize the space you use to describe your career.

You might think storytelling is a crazy strategy for your executive resume, but I assure you it is not. No hiring executive wants to know what your human resources department thinks your job should be. If you are simply describing your position, you are dulling your top-notch expertise into a simple paragraph and a few bullets that do not do your career justice.

Instead of describing the minutiae of your daily job duties, start telling stories. Your future hiring executive wants to know not what you did, but how you did it, evaluating your experience in your company and industry, not in the HR-speak of the company files. If you need a good rule of thumb, the body of your executive resume should be about 30 percent position description and 70 percent storytelling.

Follow this rubric to tell great stories. Your resume will be more interesting, and your future hiring executive will associate the problems in his or her companies with the solutions you are accustomed to driving. By answering these questions specifically, you'll choose the best parts of your career history that hiring executives and recruiters want to know. You'll demonstrate you have a proven history and strong talent for strategic leadership—and you'll show how you can hit the ground running on your first day of work.

Overall, you must deliver your career history in a series of bulleted statements that

- are factual
- are measurable
- describe not only what you did but how you did it.

Eliminate the phrase "responsible for" from your vocabulary. Instead of delivering a series of human-resources-generated statements about what you were responsible for, include powerful, goal-driven statements that uniquely describe your contributions to your company.

For each position you've held in the last ten years, include two key components: the description of your duties as well as your accomplishments. These two components are really quite different, and they serve distinct functions. Duties tell what you did; accomplishments tell why what you did was useful, valuable, and important.

Job Duties

Your job duties are, literally, the work that you do every day. Think about the work you do; now distill it to three or four sentences. Paint an accurate picture of the work you do that propels your manager, your division, or your company to rousing success.

Sample job duties for a company president or general manager might include:

- Defining company strategy.
- Increasing sales.
- Recruiting executive team and vetting hires throughout the organization.
- Reporting on financials to the executive team and board.

Job Accomplishments

Accomplishments differ radically from duties. Your accomplishments are the specific successes you've demonstrated within your job duties (or sometimes outside of them!). These show how you succeeded within your role and rose to its challenges. Unlike the duties you've specified for each role, the accomplishments tell the "so what?" about your job. They answer the question: "So what happened as a result of your work?" Usually, the answers to these questions involve some kind of metric, either numeric or evaluative, demonstrating how you improved or changed a system for the better. These accomplishments become the bullets that show why you're the most qualified to support the hiring manager's goals and needs—starting the moment you are hired.

The best way to prove you can deliver results is by providing measurements of your success—literally quantifiable numbers, metrics, KPIs (key performance indicators), or measurements of ROI (return on investment). Avenues to explore include:

- The number of projects you completed.
- The number of people you recruited (and maybe promoted).
- The number of new customers you drove to the business.
- The total dollar amount of revenues or their percentage increase quarter over quarter or year over year.

These counts or measurements of change show two things in your resume. The first is that you've accomplished the goal that you set out to, and you can benchmark those numbers against company expectations or industry standards. The second is that it shows that what you are presenting is incontrovertible evidence of your success. This is important because while a hiring manager might decide your strategies are not what their company needs, they can't argue with the veracity of your claims to success. They can't look at that number and believe that you're not telling the truth.

Because you're always telling the truth in your resume (cardinal rule of resume strategy—don't ever lie), then you are leveling with your audience. You're saying, "I did this thing, and here's the proof. Right here is the number that ways I did what I was supposed to do." If you're targeting your resume appropriately, your audience will love what you have demonstrated. If they need someone like you, you're the ideal candidate to reach out to.

So, now that you have these numbers, how do you present them effectively? These metrics become the "results" in your "challenge–action–results" bullet points. You can show them visually. The first way to do this is to list your data in a table of figures. A well-constructed table, with labels, grids, and colors, can help your audience interpret the data and understand your message the way you need them to.

Another way to represent those numbers is visually in a graph. It's so easy for someone to look at a chart and understand that the figures "go up." Your chart will be detailed, so a savvy reader who wants to drill down into the data can do that, but even a cursory glance will give a great high-level message.

You might think these are unorthodox approaches—I promise you they are not. Visual representations of sales figures that started out low and then went high or operation costs that started out higher and then went low will hit your audience right in the gut. These images are plugging into exactly what your audience expects to know about their ideal candidate. Show them what they want in multiple modalities, not just text.

Note the difference in the following examples.

Level 1: A Mere Description of Your Job, as Recorded by Human Resources

If you are an executive in charge of sales, this responsibility is likely recorded in your job description cataloged by human resources. This means you are charged with growing sales, managing a team, and leading the sales endeavor. It says nothing about whether you accomplished this goal. Therefore, at the most basic level of resume writing, you can write:

- Responsible for increasing sales.

How does such a description sound to you? Does it answer your questions about how well this person succeeded in the role? There is no context for accomplishments and no metrics by which to measure success.

Level 2: Some Context, but No Quantification

At a deeper level, you can deliver a clear description of the tactics and choices you made as an executive. More than a description of your job given by HR, you can describe the choices you made to achieve your company's goals:

- Guided sales team and drive alongs, providing coaching and mentoring to improve sales strategies and techniques.

As you can see, with more information and context, this accomplishment statement amplifies your story. It does not yet provide the metrics that describe what you did. It gets you partway, but not all the way to writing an excellent accomplishment statement.

Level 3: Context, Metrics, and Demonstration of Clear Success

At the highest level of executive resume writing, you support those accomplishments with metrics that immediately demonstrate your success. These numbers can be percentages if you are concerned about divulging company private data:

- Increased sales team's widget sales pipeline by 22 percent within two months of hire.

Sometimes, Metrics Are Not Quantifiable

What if your executive team does not measure your success with facts and figures? What if you build relationships, guide teams, and provide efficiency strategies that cannot be tied directly to specific metrics? If this is the case, then use the values by which you are judged to provide context and measurement of success. For one notable client I can recall, an internal auditing executive, his unique metrics was that his organization passed every annual audit during his tenure with the company. That's not a metric of growth or sales, but his success was critical to the company's success.

What if You Get Writer's Block?

I often hear from my executive clients that storytelling is the hardest part of their job search or resume writing process. They don't want to brag, but they also don't know how much detail to give. If you are struggling to figure out what you want to say or what you *need* to say in your resume, the following memory jobs might be very useful.

Step 1: Pick a Career Story Topic

Your story topic could be:

- What was your hardest project? What made it difficult? What did you do that made it successful?
- How did your work on a project help you or someone else do their job better?
- Of which project are you most proud? Why are you proud of it?
- How does your job differ in reality from the human resources job description you were handed when you started the position?
- What was the mess/situation/complexity that you were hired to solve?
- What was the best thing you ever did in your job—the cool outcome that makes you smile every time you recall it?
- What was the worst project you worked on? Why was it awful?
- And many more, all related to the types of problems you expect your future hiring executive to be facing (check the job posting if you are not sure what they want!).

Step 2: Tell What You Did to Fix It

In the second step, describe the action(s) you took to resolve the problem. Talk about your team's contributions, your leadership, the money you invested or saved, and the process you followed to ensure a positive outcome. For example, you might describe how you negotiated a termination clause with a vendor and brought a development team in-house for a particularly thorny project. Or you might describe the way you coached your sales team to increase top-line revenue.

Step 3: Describe the Outcome

In the final step, tell what happened in your company or your industry as a result of your contribution described in step 2. In the examples above, you might describe how bringing your development team in-house sped production 10 percent and saved the company 16 percent monthly over the original vendor cost. Or you might indicate that your sales team exceeded quota by 15 percent for three consecutive quarters and are on track for +18 percent in the current quarter.

Putting It All Together: The Accomplishment versus the Duty

In short, nobody cares that you were responsible for hiring a development team or for driving sales. At the executive level, these are part and parcel of your job, and talking about them the way your job description reads is frankly boring. If you want to wow your future hiring executive, then you need to put the bulleted statements together in a way that cannot be ignored or overlooked:

- Within 3 months of hire, jump-started flagging [project title] by exercising termination clause on expensive development vendor and recruiting five in-house developers plus project manager; completed project 10% faster than plan and saved 16% on projected budget.

- For 3 consecutive quarters, coached front-line account management team to exceed quota by 15% with combination of advanced product training and weekend retreat focused on selling strategies and customer needs assessments. On track to beat quota in Q4 20XX by 18%.

These are the accomplishment statements that impress hiring leaders. Your hiring executive needs to know not just what you did but how you did it and why it was important, and they need to know about your agency in the process. Fundamentally, if the accomplishment is relevant to a future executive role and important to you, you can and ought to tell a great story about it.

Your Education

When a client sends me a resume to review, the first thing I look at is whether they attended college. This gives me the chance to evaluate a) how much education they have strictly by the numbers, and b) how their education matches with their work experience. The reason I do this in this way is that recruiters read resumes the same way.

However, most hiring managers do not read resumes this way. In fact, they read them the same way they read anything else—from top to bottom. They start with the headline, look at a candidate's experience, and form an opinion about whether the person has the right expertise to handle the proposed job's tasks well. Eventually, they will look at the person's education and technical credentials, as these may be critical to the job candidate's ability to perform the job.

So where does education go? First or last?

First If You Are a Recent College Graduate or a Recent Graduate School Graduate

If you recently graduated from college, and the only posts you've held are typical high school and college jobs, put your education first. Most graduates do not have professional experience to speak of. What they do have going for them, however, is a college education. Highlight coursework, good grades, academic honors, and anything else that shows the level of work achieved in college. Include volunteer experience and extracurricular activities. Remember, work is work, even if it is not paid. It is still valuable and can enhance a resume.

Recent graduates with graduate-level degrees need to promote their enhanced education. This is especially true if the new degree represents a transition to a new career or industry. Like recent college graduates, those with master's-level or doctoral-level degrees should promote their academic successes first.

Last If Your Degree Is Older than One Year

Professionals and executives with a fair amount of work experience should not lead their resumes with education or training. Start with the meat of your resume—the most recent or relevant position you've held in relation to the job you are seeking. Your accomplishments and efforts are what will sell you to hiring managers and recruiters alike, not your education. A college or graduate degree might be a filter—the position may require a degree, or there may be too many applicants to wade through—so include this information, but it should be at the bottom of the last page.

The Details

List your degree (or credits earned toward the degree), your major, and your university plus city and state. But do not include the dates of your attendance or graduation. Leave off anything prior to your bachelor-level degree.

Don't Include Your High School Diploma

When your professional resume promotes your high school education, you're wasting valuable space. If you have at least one job after high school, any college education at all, or some post-high school technical training, your hiring manager is assuming that you have attended high school. What if you didn't graduate high school? I've written executive resumes for senior vice presidents who did not finish high school or who chose to complete their GED. Your chances of success aren't limited by your lack of education—in some cases, going straight to work shows an incredible work ethic. Either way, we don't need to know about your high school education, even if you never attended university.

What If I Never Went to College?

I wish I had a nickel for every time I received a call from an executive who qualifies his or her career history with, "But I never went to college." No matter what some of these people have done in their careers, how big the businesses they built became, or how much money they made, their lack of college education seems to stick in their craws. Maybe it's the one thing they could never do. Maybe it's the one thing they always wanted to do. In my experience, these executives seem to have the most amazing stories and the best experience, and all of that belongs on their executive resumes.

Rename your education section to "Executive Development," and include critical elements of training and development instead of formal education. Examples include:

- Company training programs.
- Personal development programs, such as Stephen Covey or Dale Carnegie.
- Conferences in your industry.
- Professional mentorships you delivered or took part in.
- Professional memberships, especially if you have held leadership roles.
- Any college courses you have ever taken, even if they did not result in a degree.
- Industry training programs, especially if they resulted in certifications relevant to your career goals.

Including professional training and certifications in this section highlights your commitment to continuing education without highlighting that you do not have a college degree. In fact, it sidesteps the question entirely and highlights the best of what you have done and the best of what you have learned. As a complement to your executive experience, this showcases you are an expert in your field and industry, which is really what an executive board or executive recruiter is looking for.

If a job opportunity requires a certain level of education, you may find recruiters and hiring boards will overlook your lack of college education in favor of the professional experience you bring to the table. If you're passed over for a particular role because you don't have a college degree, that company and its culture might not have been the right fit, anyway.

Promote Volunteerism

"Can I use volunteer work on a resume? Will hiring managers like what I've done, or will they consider it fluff?"

I often hear these questions from my clients. It's important to recognize that work is work, even if it's unpaid. Never lose sight of the fact that what you do every day has relevance for your job search strategy, because you're doing something important and valuable. And exploring what you like about the volunteer roles you have had can help you narrow your career.

Examples of volunteer work that can benefit your resume include:

- Sitting on the board of a non-profit institution.
- Volunteering at a church or synagogue.
- Leading programs as part of your child's PTA.
- Organizing an event, such as a food drive or fun run.
- Serving as a Boy Scout or Girl Scout guide.
- Coaching a sports team.

There are many other types of unpaid work that can bolster your job application process. The crucial thing to remember is that you must couch your leadership contributions and your accomplishments in the same way you'd account for them with your paid positions.

Volunteerism That Supports Your Return to the Workforce

You've been out of the workforce for a while due to family obligations, a layoff, a sabbatical, travel, COVID-19, or other reasons. Now it's time to get back to paid work, and you need to capture and organize your volunteer roles to showcase their value.

One key tactic in this situation is to include volunteer positions as actual in-line work experience—you're not obligated to reveal the exact amount you were paid or not paid to do the work. Each of these volunteer roles, and the promotions to leadership you might have experienced, become "jobs" in your resume, so list them exactly the same way as you detail your paid work. Make no distinction between your former paid work and your volunteer work, because they both reflect your expertise. Describing what you did every day and the successes you created are just as valuable if they prove your expertise parallels the knowledge and experience that your career target requires. Furthermore, when companies lay off employees for structural reasons—for example, COVID-induced pressures—assuring your future hiring team that you have been busy with relevant, interesting volunteer work will be an asset to your application.

To effectively describe your volunteerism, list all your volunteer roles and how you improved or added to the organization. Categories of expertise can be leadership and management, financial responsibility, operational expertise, sales of ideas/services/goods, marketing, and more. These show the knowledge and proven ability that your future audience needs to know you have, and they are subject to the challenge-action-result strategy that we've talked about before.

Volunteerism That Supplements Your Ongoing Paid Work

A second flavor of volunteerism on your resume is useful when you want to add skills and expertise that your paid work doesn't show.

Volunteer work can show the full flavor of your experience. Your professional career might be a greased rail to success but lacking a dimension you need to promote; volunteer experience demonstrates many types of expertise, not just the kind that you get paid for day to day.

Let's say you're a senior vice president of finance, and you want to show your skills in operations and team leadership so you can move into a broader role, perhaps a chief financial officer position. You might detail your recent work as the chair of a committee for a local nonprofit, a role you've held for several years. You then describe the scope and value of that work—how you fulfilled the mission of the organization through the role, how many people you guided to that goal, and how you overcame multiple challenges along the way.

Volunteer Work as the Basis for Your References

Volunteer roles can serve as a source of references for you. If you had a reporting relationship with leaders of a volunteer group, ask them for a letter of recommendation on the organization's letterhead commenting on your contributions. These people can be excellent sources of references when you need to list people who can vouch for your excellent work ethic, ability to organize projects and teams, and so on. These leaders likely will know you well and be able to describe your success and contributions to their organizations. Because you have done an incredible job, they will share a few words with your future hiring executive.

Examples of people who might serve as excellent references include:

- The executive team of the group to which you donated your time and expertise.
- Event leaders, when you directed a portion of the event.
- Co-organizers, who can comment on your excellent team spirit and ability to motivate the group.
- Your direct report team.
- A beneficiary of a nonprofit event.

To conclude, your professional paid work history is not the only work that belongs on your resume. With volunteer work, you can expand and elaborate on what makes you special and the only one who can do what you do in the way that you do it. In short, volunteer work on your professional resume enhances your brand.

Other Sections

Not every executive candidate will have foreign languages, publications, volunteer leadership, research projects, industry association memberships, and so on. If you do, title the additional section appropriately and include the relevant information. No need, however, to include anything related to personal interests or family matters.

RESUME DESIGN STRATEGIES

All resumes by qualified, certified resume writers will have the same hallmarks. They'll all have branding, keywords, and accomplishment statements in bullets. With few exceptions, they'll all be in the neighborhood of one to three pages long. And so on.

So how can you tell the difference between a ho-hum, reasonably good resume and a powerful, attention-getting, interview-winning resume? Because they have hacked the rules that govern excellent resume writing and resume design. Even if you are an executive director of art and design, the content of your resume will be paramount, with the design of your resume supporting your overall strategy.

1. Don't be afraid to mix it up with a color or two. Using color in the horizontal rules can improve the readability of your resume. Highlight important pieces of data with tasteful shading. Blues, greens, tans, and grays are all good choices. Add a pop of complementary color to highlight important information visually.

2. Include a testimonial in a text box. Use the text box function in Word to wrap your resume around a particularly laudatory comment in a letter of recommendation or annual review.

3. Create a graph or a chart to convey an increase or decrease in a critical metric—everyone understands "up" or "down" on a visceral level (consider using that touch of complementary color here).

4. Use Word's layout functions to improve your resume's readability. Put page numbers in the header or footer of your document, thus hiding them from the tracking system and promoting the readability of your resume when the system spits it out again.

5. Use horizontal rules, shading, and color appropriately. You will need to evaluate your specific industry and the expectations of your future hiring manager to determine how design-heavy you want to be. If you are applying for a marketing directorship or design leadership role, they may expect you to present a resume heavy on design. If you are applying to be a bank executive or a financial leader, plainer may be better for your specific outcomes. If you are not completely sure that using color will help, don't use any at all; you won't go wrong by being conservative in your resume design.

6. Use the right margin size. Decrease your margins from the standard 1-inch level to .5–.65 inches. The benefit is you will have more real estate to use, and your resume won't look like you styled it after a college paper.

7. Use page numbers and headers for page 2 and beyond. Headers take up space, but it would be tragic for one of your resume pages to go missing from the stack without a marker to tell its reader to which candidate it belongs. You can feel confident that a busy professional with a stack of resumes to read won't take the time to sort out which paper belongs to which candidate. Make it easy for them.

8. Don't have enough material to cover two full pages? Don't decrease your margins or drive up your font size. Instead, use judicious amounts of vertical white space to open the page up and increase its readability. While you don't have to make your resume scream in the style of John Hancock, you do want to ensure the typeface is universally available and large enough to read. Times New Roman and Arial are universal to every computer. Good and mostly universal choices also include Calibri and Cambria, Tahoma, Verdana, and Century, all in 11-point type. You may also try Arial Narrow or Garamond but use neither of these in a size smaller than 10 to 11 points. Steer clear of fonts with scrollwork or shadows; they are unprofessional and hard to read if used injudiciously and outside of heading styles.

9. Change the way executives read your resume by writing it in layers. Write your resume so that a hiring executive will see what you want him or her to see, when you want him or her to see it. Start by designing your resume so the hiring executive reads the branding first. Then construct your resume using as many as two layers of headings and two layers of bullets. This allows a high-level read and multiple levels of deeper reads, enabling your hiring executive to dig deeper into your content and to get more and more information about your candidacy with each review.

Readability of the document itself can be as important as its contents. If a hiring manager finds your resume hard to read, they'll put it aside because it doesn't match the expectations for usability. Don't let yours be consigned to the trash simply because you didn't consider its presentation.

RESUME LENGTH

Job seekers with long careers tend to have had . . . long careers. When they are ready to write their resumes, they want to include the best and the greatest experience. Instead, they choose to start with their very first job, making their resume span multiple decades. The result is a long, directionless document. The right length for your executive resume is as long as it takes to successfully describe your career accomplishments so that your future hiring executive completely understands why you're the right candidate.

Resume Length for Individual Contributors

Base the length of your resume on the depth of your own experience. If you are an individual contributor, promoting in depth the last ten years of your professional experience is sufficient. You can show growth and progression in your career in that amount of time. Two pages is a good rule of thumb. If your last ten years of work was with the same organization, one page might very well support your entire career history.

Resume Length for Managers

As you grew from the level of an individual contributor to a leadership position, the flavor of your professional contribution changed. If you are seeking another management-level position, balance the ten-year rule of thumb with the titles you've recently held. To brand yourself according to your most recent titles, you might focus in depth only on the last eight years—or perhaps the last fifteen. Avoid highlighting lower-level positions that don't support your future goals, except if they provided you the platform and the technical experience to launch your management career.

Resume Length for Executives

If you are an executive, balance the ten-year rule of thumb with the titles you have had. If you're a president now, and over the last fifteen years, your titles were vice president, senior director, and director, you might focus on your president and vice president roles in depth, relegating your earlier and lower-level experience to a smaller proportion of the resume real estate. The optimal length of your resume should be two to three full pages.

PROOFREAD!

Do not hit "send" before you check and recheck your resume, cover letter, and email, or you will suffer the red-faced embarrassment of regret and self-recrimination.

Follow this checklist to make sure every element is pixel-perfect:

Check Your Resume Header for Mistakes In:

- Your first name
- Your last name
- Your phone number
- Your address, city, state, and ZIP code
- Your headline (does it match your specific job target?)
- Your branding (does it reflect the needs of your audience?)

Check Your Resume Overall For:

- Indents and alignments
- Font sizes and typefaces
- Widows and orphans
- Document format (.doc? .docx? .rtf? .pdf?)
- Misspellings
- Extra spaces where they do not belong (there is ONE space after a period!)

Check Your Cover Letter Email For:

- Correct spelling of the addressee
- Correct email of the addressee
- Right company name
- Proper job title

- Correct date
- Proper document(s) attached

Once you have checked every element of your resume and cover letter, check them again with my super-secret weapon that helps you find your hidden errors, even when you have read your resume eighteen times (once for each of the above tips) or more:

- Read the document backward
- Start with the last sentence
- Read it aloud
- Check for errors
- Move on to the prior sentence
- Repeat
- Best Editorial Tip

If there is any doubt about the veracity or level of appropriateness of your email, DO NOT SEND IT. You will regret sending the wrong sort of message, particularly if what you intend to be funny becomes insulting or inappropriate to your audience.

— 7 —
WRITING AN EXCEPTIONAL COVER LETTER

COVER LETTERS ARE CRUCIAL

THE WORLD IS BINARY, as the humorous quote states: "There are only 10 types of people in the world: Those who understand binary, and those who don't." It's also divided into hiring managers who love cover letters and those who hate them.

Which type of hiring manager are you speaking to when you submit your resume? The answer is, *you don't know*. This means you have to submit your resume with a cover letter that sings. Every time. No exceptions. Starting now. Including a cover letter is more than a professional courtesy: It gives the resume context and explains to the hiring manager why you are sending a resume.

NEVER SEND A NAKED RESUME

If we assume that the audience for your executive resume is human, then cover letters have two targets: one is people who read cover letters, and the other is people who don't. What does this mean for your application? You don't know if your audience will read your resume, so if there is even a slight chance they'll read your letter, then you better make it a good one.

What makes an excellent cover letter? First, it is not a generic, "Here I am, and I'm ready to apply for this job. I read online that there's this job available, and you could consider me." That message is detached and bland. To get more personal and ensure your letter resonates with your audience, think about what the job specifically is asking for and infuse some of your background regarding your audience's expectations in this cover letter.

As you mention relevant points from your executive career history, highlight the key achievements that you think will apply to this audience—in the context of what this company is expecting. So don't even start to put pen to paper until you have done some research on the company and the role and have thought about culture fit, language choice, and all the factors that will appeal to your audience.

Recently, I was writing a cover letter for an outside sales leader. The job posting was revealing. The language was something like this: "Have tattoos? Great! Show off your ink. Like to come in with pink hair? Great! We love color." Clearly, this audience is a bit looser, friendlier, less buttoned-up than, say, a company that merely says, "Sales leader required." You can learn more about the company culture, beyond how the job posting reads, on the company website, specifically in the "about us" section.

Other key elements you need to include in your cover letter, typically after you describe your expertise, are the two "asks." Your cover letter introduces your resume, so you want to invite your reader a) to look at your resume for additional information, and b) to ask for the interview. You don't ask for the interview because it's expected; you ask for it because it matters to you, and you want your audience to connect with the fact that you care about getting this interview.

Overall, you have a cover letter because you don't know if your audience will read it or not; you know not to send a naked resume. As you prepare your letter, always let them know you are passionate about what you are asking for, because your enthusiasm for the role will be critical to their interpretation of your candidacy.

It should be noted that cover letters shouldn't make applicants sound whiny: "I want, and I want, and I want, and you should" is not how a cover letter should read. The letter should be all about the company's needs, and very little about the applicant's wants or desires—except about how the applicant's goal is to exceed all the company's needs and requirements. The applicant would be better served to say that she has done X, Y, and Z before, and she can do it again.

In short, it's not about what the company can do for you and how it can support your goals. It is about how you, the applicant, can improve the company in so many ways.

QUALITIES OF A GREAT COVER LETTER

A Great Cover Letter Doesn't Bore or Antagonize

Your cover letter is not about you, at least not to start. Your cover letter is about what you can do for the company to which you are applying. Tell the hiring manager why you understand the company's situation or position. Explain what you bring that is unique and essential to the position. Capitalize on the hiring manager's need to hire someone they don't have to train and who can hit the ground running.

Don't whine, demand, or convey in any way that you need something from the company. Don't be rude or childish in your prose. Don't be too personal, and don't use instant-messaging speak (e.g., "CU l8r" is great for your pals, but it makes a terrible impression on a professional). In other words, don't give the reader a reason to reject your letter out of hand.

Your professional resume writer understands the correct language, tone, and presentation for your cover letter. She will demonstrate your keen industry understanding in an inviting, carefully worded manner. She knows your industry well, so she'll select timely business topics that are relevant and interesting to the hiring manager.

A Great Cover Letter Is Thought-Provoking

A great cover letter presents your qualifications in light of the company's needs, not the other way around (again: the company doesn't care about your needs, wants, or aspirations). Make the recruiter think you are the right person for the job. You can do this by presenting a thought-provoking statement about the industry, or even a contradiction that only you, with your brilliant career, can untangle for the reader.

The writing professional you select should be able to craft a document that hooks the hiring manager instantly. She'll show a bit of creativity on your behalf, using your branding and industry expertise as the basis for a structured introduction that will have the hiring manager nodding in agreement with your perspective.

A Great Cover Letter Functions as an Advertisement for Your Resume

The subsequent paragraphs or bullets should reflect your amazing expertise. You have less than ten seconds to convince the hiring manager to put your resume into the "call for interview" pile. A good resume/cover letter writer will select the best of your accomplishments and craft vibrant achievement statements that reflect the specific position—without rewriting or copying your resume.

A Great Cover Letter Asks for the Interview

You've heard this phrase: "You get what you ask for." The flip side is also true. You *won't* get what you *don't* ask for, particularly in the context of the ask for the interview. In that sense, your cover letter, your initial communication with a hiring manager, should clearly ask for a meeting during which you can elaborate on your unique skills sets.

COVER LETTER TEMPLATES FAIL

I am constantly amazed by the cover letter templates on sites purporting to deliver expert advice. I did a quick Google search for "free cover letter sample." The sample letters I dug up missed major opportunities to rise to the top of the stack. Primarily, they're extremely generic. They don't set the focus outward onto ways the applicant can solve the hiring manager's pain. And they don't ask for the interview.

When you present unassuming, generic language in your letter to a hiring manager, you're presenting yourself as unfocused and unsure of your goal. In the current economy, where unemployment rates drive up applications for coveted spots, the hiring manager will not take the time to figure out what you can offer. It's up to you to state clearly your expertise—and your desire to meet this hiring manager for this position. You'll sound educated about the potential role and focused about your ambitions.

DON'T MISS AN OPPORTUNITY TO USE YOUR COVER LETTER EFFECTIVELY

Every word on your resume counts—it's the same for your cover letter. Don't miss the opportunity to ask for what you want. Don't expect the reader to assume that you're the most eager, the best qualified, and the most likely to succeed in the position. Give them what they need to draw your resume out the stack: a sharply presented, clearly stated request for the interview. After all, this is the point of your resume/cover letter package—to get you in for a face-to-face so you can show the hiring manager that you will succeed in your target role.

FORMAT OF A GREAT COVER LETTER

Your Strategy for Catching a Hiring Manager's Attention

You can search the web for samples—but they won't always be right for your job search. Some are of the "please read my attached resume" variety, and those will simply bore your reader.

As you read these resume and samples them, look for the following format:

1. **Standard letter-writing format.** Include a header with your address and contact information.

2. **Individual addressee.** Don't embarrass yourself and automatically consign your resume to the dustbin by neglecting to personalize your letter for the hiring manager and position you're seeking.

3. **Proper salutation.** Address your reader formally with "Dear Ms. Smith," or if you don't know the hiring manager's name, "Dear Hiring Manager." "To whom it may concern" is strikingly impersonal, and "Dear Scott" is too informal, even if you know the hiring manager personally.

4. **Clever opening paragraph.** This is the hardest part of the cover letter. Tactics you can try include:

    - Invite the reader to join you in thinking about something related to the industry.

    - Make a bold statement, and then defend it using your experience as an example.

    - Make a bold statement and then refute it, using your history to disprove it.

Whatever you do, catch your reader's attention and hold it. Make him want to read your resume, pick up the phone, and call you for an interview.

5. **Relevant accomplishments.** Use a bulleted list if you want to highlight three or more accomplishments. Use a paragraph if you're a recent graduate or want to tell a story rather than simply highlight facts. Don't copy and paste your resume.

6. **Interview ask.** Close your letter with a request for the interview. Again, you won't get what you don't ask for.

7. **One page.** Again, your letter is a teaser for your resume. If you've gone over one page, you're boring your reader. Be succinct; be punchy; be powerful. Remember, attention spans for emails are shorter than those for printed material. Your emailed cover letter might be half to two-thirds the length of your printed one.

8. **Impeccable grammar and spelling.** If this isn't your long suit, ask someone to read it. Barring that, read it out loud to yourself. Backward. Sentence by sentence. Trust me: that technique will enable you to focus on each word of each sentence.

9. **Close your letter respectfully, but not too personally.** "Sincerely" always works. "Yours truly" seems a bit intimate for your job search.

10. **Hire an expert writer if you have any misgivings.** If you have any reservations about your ability to craft a top-flight resume, cover letter, or post-interview thank you letter, hire a certified advanced resume writer. No doubt you'll shorten your job search.

SAMPLE RESUMES AND COVER LETTERS

Ever wonder why it's so difficult to find good sample resumes and cover letters out there on the internet? Do a Google search, and you'll get millions of options. How do you know that the site you're viewing can help you get the interview you need for the job you want?

A Good Sample Resume Has Three Critical Elements:

1. It's a real resume with noncritical details fictionalized for the sake of the actual job seeker's privacy. A real resume that got a real interview has inherent credibility and value.

2. An industry expert wrote it. Check the writer's credentials for certifications, experience, and track record. Look at the person's testimonials and success stories—mine, for example, are actual quotes from satisfied job-seeking clients.

3. A successful sample resume follows industry standards. Your human audience needs to understand your goals and intentions for your new position. Searchers on corporate applicant tracking systems, into which you upload your resume and cover letter, need to find your resume easily among the thousands stored there.

A Good Sample Cover Letter Also Follows Three Essential Requirements:

1. A superior cover letter sample is a real document (fictionalized for privacy), and its style matches its associated resume. They form a complete package that addresses the (very real) hiring team's (very specific) needs.

2. A great sample cover letter shows you how to address the job target and job description. By using language that the hiring team expects to see, this letter addresses specific points related to the job target, showing that the applicant is competent, skilled, and knowledgeable.

3. Last, a cover letter, after which you can model your own, sounds like the person for whom it was written. When you model your cover letter (or resume) after a sample you read, use language that sounds like you, not like the person about whom it was written. Just as a good sample resume and cover letter go together in style and format, ensure that your resume and cover letter feel like they match.

— 8 —

EXECUTIVE RESUME WRITING FOR ENTREPRENEURS

CONSTRUCTING YOUR STORY FOR THE CORPORATE WORLD

IN A TOUGH ECONOMY, when small businesses thrive, it's due to their team strategy, marketing, and more—including their executive leadership. These entrepreneurs are the power on which our successful economy rests. If you're an entrepreneur who has exited your small business, you need to know how your skills and assets can impress a hiring manager.

You—a current or former business owner—need to convince a hiring manager that:

1. You're an executive ready to lead the charge to a company's profitability.
2. You're a professional who can follow the beat of someone else's drum—maybe for the first time in your professional career.

No matter whether you're a mid-career professional or a true executive, you need to prove:

1. You are ready to give up the powerful independent life.
2. You're ready to throw your lot in with the rest of the professional world.
3. You're ready to work with others on teams.

4. You're ready to take direction from someone who might not have the same perspective—or experience—as you.

The Answer

You need an entrepreneur resume. Resumes for entrepreneurs are substantively different from standard business resumes.

If you're a business owner, you're probably smart, driven, customer-oriented, and proud of your ability to do whatever it is your company does. You might have an MBA, or you might have just made it through high school. You might have been working for your own enterprise for five months, five years, or twenty-five years. In any case, you're thinking it's time to leave the business in someone else's hands or close it altogether.

You may not have written a resume before—your company was flying high, and you've enjoyed the responsibility, pressure, and elation of success. But if you're ready to take the plunge, your entrepreneur resume has to show some serious innovation and expertise. You need to blow the competition away, but you'll be competing with all other comers on their terms, which might be substantially different from the ones that have driven your success in the past.

HOW TO APPROACH YOUR RESUME WHEN YOU'RE AN ENTREPRENEUR

Let's face it. In the entrepreneurial space: no guts, no glory. So, what happens when you consider moving into the corporate world after a few years—or even a few decades? What do you need to include on your resume to bring it up to date historically and strategically? Strategies for resume writing have transformed since you last looked for a job. Thus, the resume that got you your first position is not likely going to support your latest job search.

Don't Write an Objective Statement

As a job seeker, you're at a disadvantage in the power structure between you and your future hiring manager. Now is not the time to demand anything of someone whose support you need. Replace an objective statement with a powerful description of your entrepreneurial professional brand. Make your reader want to meet you, the wise and experienced entrepreneur.

Highlight Your Accomplishments

Accomplishments in a resume for entrepreneurs are critical. By showing what you have accomplished in the past, you will show a hiring manager that you can achieve the same goals for his or her company. For example, demonstrate that you're the right one for the job due to your incredible track record of high sales, decreased turnover, technical expertise, or human resources talent.

Talk about Teamwork

First, emphasize any team projects you've taken part in within your business, whether with subordinates, other industry players, or clients. Ensure your prospective hiring manager knows you're a team player, and you aren't afraid to collaborate.

Show Increasing Levels of Responsibility

Even within your own company, you probably started with smaller projects and worked your way to bigger ones. Excellent challenge-action-response statements will show how you wrangled the most success from sticky situations. These will resemble the problems hiring managers are desperate to solve.

Write for Your Audience

Demonstrate your growth with strong action words and as many quantitative and qualitative assessments as you can. Pick powerful language; don't use boring text that doesn't grab attention.

Don't Hold Yourself to the One-Page Rule for Your Entrepreneur Resume

If you have been working for twenty years, much of those in senior positions, you will have excellent stories to tell. Amplify those accomplishments and feel confident that two or even three pages is acceptable for resume length now, as long as you use your resume real estate wisely.

Don't Say References Are Available on Request

Your future hiring leader knows this—all good candidates have a list of people on whom they can call to vouch for their professional excellence. Having references is a given, so use your resume real estate to promote your expertise instead. Remember to print out a list of your references on a separate page, however, so you can offer it during an interview.

Don't Worry about Your Formal Education—or Lack of It

If you chose the entrepreneurial route rather than higher education, stop worrying about its absence on your resume. You can't change the past, and you don't have to. Your experience, properly conveyed on paper with powerful accomplishment statements about your expertise, will tell a much better story. If it's always been your lifelong goal to complete college, don't let time stand in your way. But know that your resume will soar when you describe the amazing work you've done as a successful entrepreneur.

Brush Up Your Word Processing Skills to Create Your New Resume

If you're not sure how to use Word, which is the word processing gold standard, take a community education class—or hire a virtual assistant to do the typing.

Hire a Professional Resume Writing Service

When you were out pounding the pavement as the leader of your own company, you made sure that your clients knew they were hiring an expert. If you're stuck about what to say in your resume, you, too, can hire an expert.

THE EXECUTIVE BIOGRAPHY

What Is It?

A professional biography is not a resume. It's a one-page statement of who you are from a branding perspective—a marketing document that is content-heavy, attractive, and readable. Its purpose is to convince a hiring manager that you have the substance and experience to make interviewing you worth their while.

Constructing a Professional Bio from the Ground Up

You probably feel like your business is your life. But your business owner experience is not the same as your life story. Your professional biography will probably start somewhere around the time you developed your idea for your company. If that was while you were in college, great, use that to your advantage. While this document is called a biography, it doesn't mean you recount your personal history starting from your childhood. Remember, everything you present to a future hiring manager counts, and this needs to be clean, professional, content-laden, and well-written to get a jaded hiring manager's attention.

Key Sections of a Professional Biography

Many formats will work for a professional bio; research what your potential colleagues have developed. Likely they will all contain the following elements:

- A history of how you got to where you are seeking to transition to corporate life.
- A brief discussion of your skill set, detailing a few stories of accomplishments specifically related to your target role.
- Your educational history.
- Your contact information.
- Your photo, if you choose.
- Recommendations or testimonials from clients and vendors.
- Speaking engagements or publications related to your industry.
- Related interests and hobbies, if appropriate.

How to Use a Professional Biography

Certainly, you must have a resume if you are applying for jobs. However, as you network into companies and work with recruiters, you might want to have copies of your professional biography ready to present. Because your bio will be lighter and eminently readable yet still contain the essential elements of your brand, recruiters and hiring managers can use it to get a broader sense of the person behind the words—you, the professional, ready to tackle corporate positions successfully.

WHAT IF YOU FAILED AS AN ENTREPRENEUR? WHERE DOES *THAT* GO ON YOUR RESUME?

What if you were part of a failed start-up, and there is nothing representative of your accomplishments to report on your resume? This can be an extraordinarily tough situation for former entrepreneurs to negotiate. The trick to creating a successful entrepreneur resume is to focus on the key contributions that you made, even if they did not ultimately result in a profitable conclusion. The accomplishment is in initiating and succeeding through the process, not its result.

Your resume would ideally publicize the incredible accomplishments that you have produced for your company. For example, you might mention:

- You generated sales growth of 12 percent YOY 2015–2020.
- You promoted eight people on your team to management positions.
- You closed six new high-profile clients.

But what if you can't lay claim to any of them, because your entrepreneurial venture failed? To include this span of experience in which you do not have traditional accomplishments to report, start with what you did well. Instead of taking the traditional approach to resume writing, which focuses on end results, focus on the processes you began and continued with throughout your experience in the entrepreneurial environment.

For example, you might mention the innovative ways:

- You started a company, either on your own or with others.
- You achieved financial backing.
- You set up operations, and you began a production process.
- You initiated sales.
- You consulted with clients.

Your overall goal is to focus not on the company's successes as a measure of your own but on the initiative and programs unique to your effort and vision. Reflect on the good that you did because of your entrepreneurship, and craft the resume around your ability to establish and fulfill processes whose end might be more profitable in another, perhaps more stable growth-oriented organization that requires your brand of innovation.

— 9 —

WORKING WITH A RESUME WRITING SERVICE

HOW TO CHOOSE AN EXECUTIVE RESUME WRITING SERVICE

THE CHALLENGE OF WRITING your executive resume often breaks down into two options: Either you write it yourself or you choose a resume writing service that will advance your job search strategy for you.

There is no single list that will satisfy all your expectations for the ideal executive resume writing provider. You, as the consumer, have to choose, knowing that the ranking systems are so often skewed by their authors and adjudicators. Choose your executive resume service wisely, according to all that you know about yourself and your unique career management needs.

Look at Location

You might want a resume writing service local to your home city, but if location doesn't matter, then choose a reputable one from across the globe. However, a resume writer should never claim to be #1 in a market in which he or she does not live and work—doing so would be false advertising and presenting a false credential to the public.

Look for Experience

The first filter you should use when evaluating an executive resume writing service is the level of experience that service or that individual has with writing executive resumes. There are perhaps thousands of resume writers, but most do not work at the executive level. Expert resume writers are accustomed to working with and catering to individuals with little time, high expectations, long careers, and complex career histories.

Look for Credentials

The resume writing industry offers several credentials and certifications. The most basic resume writing credentials include Certified Advanced Resume Writer (Career Directors International), Academy Certified Resume Writer (Resume Writing Academy), Nationally Certified Resume Writer (National Resume Writers Association), and Certified Professional Resume Writer (Professional Association of Resume Writers and Career Coaches). Being recognized with one of these resume writing certifications means that the resume writer has a certain level of experience and training, plus that the person's work is evaluated and certified by experts in the industry. A company that self-designates its writers with a homegrown "certification" might or might not be up to the standards of the industry.

Look for Awards

The main resume writing competition, held annually, is the Toast of the Resume Industry Awards, commonly known as the TORIs. Each year, Career Directors International invites entrants to compete in nine categories. In the spring, it names five nominees, and by summer it names first, second, and third for each category. Entries are evaluated in a two-layer, blind process by the most senior professionals in the industry, and thus the competition has a great deal of credibility. Review the profiles and winning entries for the Best Executive Resume categories in the TORIs of recent years. I won first place for Best Executive Resume a number of years ago, which was a lot like winning a resume Oscar. I served as a judge for a few years as well, so I have deep insight into what it's like to win and into the delight of evaluating others' work.

In recent years, there have been reports of self-styled awards and top-10 rankings that organizations give to themselves, likely to bolster their internet presence. Be wise and wary of a company that places itself first among its colleagues, and do your homework to determine whether a company's badges and awards are conveyed by a reputable resource.

Look for Testimonials

Both the LinkedIn profiles and the websites of experienced executive resume writers should contain unsolicited testimonials from happy clients. In fact, these testimonials might be the only references you can get from reputable resume writers. Experienced executive resume writers rarely provide the names and contact information of their clients, as they protect their high-profile clients' identities. If they protect those clients, you can expect them to protect your confidentiality. You might find testimonials on the resume writer's website and on their LinkedIn profile (pro tip: LinkedIn recommendations come with names attached—look at their profiles to see if you like the writer's style). Third-party reviewing sites are less trustworthy, so treat what you read there with a grain of salt, as are reviews by internal employees.

Pricing

In the resume writing industry, training and expertise take a great deal of time. Typically, those in business for just a few years charge low rates because they have not put in their ten thousand hours of practice and training to become an expert in the field. Those who consider themselves experts in executive resume writing should be able to prove that they have years of editorial experience, recruiting, human resources, and the certifications and credentials that go with the coveted designation of "executive resume writer."

Individual Practitioner or Agency Leadership

Executive resume writing companies come in two flavors: Individual practitioners and agency models. Individual practitioners run their business and engage with their clients on all aspects of the development of their career portfolios. Agency model owners have often been resume writers and recruiters themselves, holding the proper certifications, but now lead an expert writing team providing individual services. Both are valuable and respected within the industry. When the owner or individual practitioner knows a great deal about each client and adds their expertise to that client's strategy, the result is bound to be more effective.

Unfortunately, agency models in which the leader or owner is inexperienced, detached from the business because of lack of experience or knowledge, or simply not an experienced professional may offer little recourse if your resume writer fails to deliver on your strategy.

Credible Web Presence

Experienced executive resume writers have great websites. They are informative and honestly describe the writer's experience, expertise, and ideal client. They do not boast about being #1 in markets and functions in which they do not have experience, although they often are proud to provide links to the professional societies with which they have standing, awards, or credentials. They have very real testimonials (sometimes anonymized to protect client identity), and photos can be reverse-searched on Google Images to reveal their veracity. Video testimonials should also present actual clients.

Ethical Behavior and Honesty in Resume Writing Practice

Perhaps most important of all of these is a commitment to ethics and honesty in the practice of resume writing. Ethical practice and honesty take a few forms:

- Refraining from offering a guarantee, for example, for interviews or a job to which the service cannot possibly commit.
- Avoiding proclamations of expertise without credible corroboration.
- A deep pride in very real expertise and honest humility when a client asks for a service outside the provider's ability (this provider should recommend a colleague, by name, with the right expertise if the situation warrants it).

Where NOT to Look for an Executive Resume Writer

As you search the web for executive resume writers, you might find the "Top 10 Resume Writing Sites" or broad services that cater to clients at every level. These won't be the right providers for an executive who expects white-glove service. Internet ads for $50 or $100 are probably not the right choice either; these might turn out to be little more than typing services that reformat your existing content rather than develop your unique selling proposition.

Seek the Right Fit

Credentialed executive resume writers serve the unique needs of an expert population. If you're looking for top talent, don't settle for the lowest-priced provider. Look beyond price to the value of hiring an expert who will challenge you to think deeply about your career, including your history and your goals. If they don't motivate you to explore your path ahead, then perhaps that person is not right for you. If you have chosen wisely, your resume writer

- should treat you amicably and respectfully—you feel at ease talking to them as an expert on your own history and as a partner in the process
- should be comfortable discussing (read: understand) complicated career stories
- should lay out their plan that relies on tested resume writing techniques and, when warranted, infuses a layer of strategy that is unique to your specific situation
- will do everything possible to learn as much as they can about you in conversations, written responses, and ongoing discussions (for which you will have their direct contact information, gladly provided for just this purpose)
- will speak honestly with you about the revisions you recommend—most professional resume writers are more than willing to consider and/or incorporate revisions, so long as they are strategically sound
- should adhere to their customary strategy while accommodating, within reason, your particular needs for meeting times, response times, and strategic determinations that advance your career trajectory.

For your collaboration with your executive resume writer to be successful, you will have to commit to the following principles:

- Communication
- Vulnerability
- Honesty
- Pride
- Humility
- Collaboration

In fact, your executive resume is likely to be even better than you imagined if you collaborate extensively on the first draft. When you are reading that first draft, you might find that you want to tweak the phrasing, add something, or challenge what your resume writer put to paper.

DO IT!

Resume writers with long and deep editorial careers can take it—and they want you to collaborate. Bring your best; you will not regret it.

Even if you are not an executive, but especially if you are, there are multiple litmus tests you can use to determine whether you've made the right choice. Don't be afraid to do your due diligence, and never agree to hire an unknown professional strictly based on low cost.

WHY CHOOSE A RESUME WRITER? YOU DON'T KNOW WHAT YOU KNOW ABOUT YOURSELF

An Executive Resume Writer Is Your Guide

When you meet your executive resume writer for the first time, you can expect a bit of an introduction, some small talk, some discussion about the process. You'll mention your industry and your current job. Your resume writer doesn't know you, and you might worry about how, inside an hour or two, this person will know you well enough to write effectively for you.

A resume writer's ability to do exactly that is what makes her great. Resume writing is about the writing, for sure. More than that, it's about asking the right questions and listening.

Your professional resume writer will know how to ask the right questions that will uncover all of your great accomplishments. And she'll figure out things about you that you didn't know about yourself.

The Resume Inquiry Process

Your resume writer probably has a set of stock questions that she will ask you to get the process started. These might include:

- What kind of position are you seeking?
- What industry are you interested in working in?
- How many years have you been planning this kind of career move?

These questions frame the discussion that will lead to your amazing career documentation.

The program that I developed over years incorporates these and dozens more questions that elicit the best of what my clients want to tell their future hiring teams. My clients uniformly tell me that the work is hard but worth it. If your resume writer is not asking you sufficient (or any) questions, ask for a refund. They will not learn anything new about you, and your resources (time, money, headaches) will be wasted.

Getting the Very Best from You

The next set of questions relate to each position you've held. If your resume is like the hundreds that have crossed my desk, it will do a fantastic job of . . . reporting. I read the *whos*, the *whats*, and the *whens*. These types of resumes tell a pretty good narrative for each job and tell a recruiter what a candidate did every day—which is *not* what he wants to read.

A recruiter wants to read the *whys* in a resume. And the *hows*. And the *what happened nexts*. Your professional resume writer knows how to generate these questions so they are specific to your particular job level, industry, and even region and demographic.

What Are Your Questions?

I can't write here what the questions would be for your specific situation and career aspirations—I haven't met you yet. But if we ever speak about your history, I'll have all the right questions on the tip of my tongue. And you'll be surprised when you hear your answers. I'll bet you didn't know what you knew about yourself.

PART 3

NETWORK

— 10 —
CONNECT FOR SUCCESS

JOB SEEKERS SUCCEED WHEN THEY NETWORK

WHAT DO YOU THINK the key to savvy executive job search is? Is it your resume, your interview, or your LinkedIn profile? The answer might surprise you. The key to your executive job search is your recommendation by a current employee of the company you are targeting.

To be successful as you network, you must find the hidden, unadvertised job market and use every resource available to you. Networking, when done correctly, will lead to plentiful contacts and friendships that can help you in every aspect of your career, including job hunting and your future career endeavors. It can prove to be more important than any other facet of your search.

Before Networking—Review Your Goals

What do you want others to know about you? What do you need to learn from them?

1. What kind of job are you looking for?
2. Do you want to look for jobs in one city/state?
3. Are you focused on a certain industry?

4. Do you want to find a job at a particular company?

5. Have you attained the skills and experience required for this position?

6. Effective Networking Strategies

When starting out, remember, it's never about blatantly asking for a job. It's about talking things over one-on-one with someone you know (or someone referred to you) about common interests and how you might help them and their company.

Before diving into a lengthy narrative about yourself, be sure to ask common questions to get warmed up. Ask about family, friends, interests—topics that you wouldn't mind discussing yourself. Once the conversation is flowing, you can shift gears to the actual reason for the call:

"I'm calling because I'm planning to make a job change soon. I am looking for a new opportunity that will both challenge and expand my skill set. Do you know anyone who works within my target field who might lead me in the right direction?"

Using this simple script as a guide may give you the confidence you need to open up and freely discuss options and career paths that may be available to you.

Career Networking Tips

1. Create an inventory of your educational background, accomplishments, and work history. You never know when a casual interaction may lead to a contact.

2. Your career network should include, but not be limited to, family, friends, members of neighborhood associations, past or present coworkers, supervisors, and colleagues from other business connections. If you are part of an alumni club from your college or university, you may also find leads there.

3. Use sites like LinkedIn, Facebook, and other online communities can help you get in touch with other networkers. Maybe those with college affiliations or who are in a certain geographic area. Also, keep in touch with your network often. This can be as simple as sending a quick note or email to say hello and to ask how they are doing. You want to make an impression and be remembered.

4. Attend networking events. If you belong to any professional associations, attend a meeting or social function. Many of the attendees will have the same goals you do and will be glad to exchange information.

5. Add notes to business cards or organize electronically so you'll remember the details of whom you have just met. Also, follow through with referrals, and always thank contacts in writing or email.

HOW YOUR INSIDE CONNECTION LEADS TO YOUR NEXT EXECUTIVE ROLE

Networking Is the Best Way to Learn about New Positions

Even though job-search networking may sound intimidating, it is one of the most successful ways to find a new job. It is more common than you realize to be offered a job or to find a contact simply due to a friend or acquaintance knowing your background and skills. If you are serious about finding the best position for your next career, move as quickly as possible; you must reach out and network.

Connections inside the Company Give You the Advantage

Ask an influential current employee of your target company to recommend you to the hiring executive.

The inside connection will make or break your executive job search. In fact, according to leading industry experts, if you don't have an advocate inside the company, you might as well not apply for the position at all. It's considered a fact of life that hiring executives won't look among the hundreds to thousands of resumes they receive for each open role—they'll look at as many as they need to fill the available interview slots.

How the Referral Process Works

A position is posted, and the applicant tracking system or web application site receives 150 resumes. For the sake of argument, we can assume that half of those are not qualified for the role.

Recruiters regularly lament the fact that they receive resumes all the time from candidates who match only some of the qualifications. The moral of this story is that executives need to read the job description carefully to make sure they fit all the qualifications and requirements for the role. Remember, the interview is about fit, not about qualifications, so do not be lulled into a false sense of security because you are smart (you are), experienced (you have years), and a quick learner (that is not a qualification for anything). You need to show right from the start that you have experience in all facets of the role.

So, of our 150 applicants, seventy-five are not qualified, and seventy-five are. At the same time that resumes are rolling in through the online application system, five smart executives have been making connections within the company, and they each have been speaking to influential employees. These five current employees have passed these five resumes to the executive decision maker.

Let's also say that the applicant tracking system and the internal recruiter choose the top several of the resumes that come through the online job site; however, the executive receiving referrals from trusted employees pushes one or two (if not all five) of the resumes he or she received to the top of the list. Thus, the former five top resumes that came in through the system are now three or four, because the referrals from trusted insiders edged out the bottom few from the original list.

Why Recommendations Matter and What You Need to Do about It

There is no question that referrals and recommendations from existing employees truly count. Those qualified candidates from the list of referrals now have a one in five (total interview slots) chance of receiving an offer, which far outpaces the one in seventy-five of fundamentally qualified candidates. The math prevails, and referrals now truly count.

You can become one of the top referral candidates by engaging in a concentrated networking strategy that makes you into a name with a face, qualifications, personality, and experience. By creating trustworthy connections within your targeted company list, you can increase your chances of being selected for an executive role from one in hundreds to one in a handful.

THREE NETWORKING MYTHS THAT HURT YOUR CAREER GROWTH

When it comes to networking, executives tend to fall into two camps. They either love to network or they ignore it. Perhaps executives who don't consciously maintain their networks have fallen for one of these three top myths about networking.

Myth #1: Networking Is for Job Search Only

When looking for a job, you are wise to reach out to connections, and perhaps you made some interesting connections the last time you were in a job search. However, the most common error executives make when they transition to new roles is failing to maintain the connections they have built. You might have a list of great contacts with whom you have not spoken in several years, too.

Executives (job seekers at every level, actually) must remember that the network they built throughout their search needs nurturing even after they get the job. These are the people whom executives can ask for advice, meet at industry conferences, and recommend for future roles within their own companies.

Myth #2: Networking Is for Extroverts Only

Introverts are often given short shrift around networking. Extroverts paint introverts as shy, retiring, or even misanthropic, when, in fact, the opposite is often true. These individuals are thoughtful and enjoy one-on-one conversations, which is what meaningful networking truly is. Introverted executives can capitalize on their strengths of engaging in intensive listening, learning, and advising in small-group conversations—all components of a powerful networking strategy that have nothing to do with sharing what they perceive to be insipid small talk over the punch bowl at a large business event.

Myth #3: Networking Means Constantly Finding New People to Talk To

Networking is not only about increasing the number of people you know. In fact, effective networking is more about deepening the good relationships executives already have, if those relationships are the right ones to solve the particular question. Therefore, rather than seek to expand the breadth of the network, executives might start with the people they know best and keep those relationships warm over months or years. These professional friendships are valuable when executives find that they have job-search or career-advancement questions and needs. They are part of a trusted network that now has deep roots based on time-tested mutual trust.

MEASURE YOUR JOB SEARCH NETWORKING SUCCESS

While you are in the midst of networking, the process can seem thankless. Do you wonder whether you are really getting anywhere with your networking strategy? Did that connection you made a month ago turn into something? How do you know whether the presentation you attended was worth going to from a networking perspective? Although it is hard to pin job search success onto any one networking event, overall, you can measure your networking success with a few simple metrics.

New Connections on LinkedIn

When you collect business cards at a networking event, do you turn them into LinkedIn connections? If not, you are missing a tremendous opportunity to broaden your network. Measure the growth of your first-degree connections—those you have met in person and those you "meet" virtually—to see whether your networking efforts are bearing fruit.

Telephone Meetings

Often, first-degree connections on LinkedIn linger in purgatory, never becoming real-world connections with whom you have conversations. How many of these first-degree connections result in telephone conversations, during which you can ask your new contact a variety of questions about their experiences, positions, companies, and industries? If your number is small, you might need to open this bottleneck in the networking process.

Face-to-Face Meetings

How many of your telephone conversations turn into real-world meetings? The face-to-face meeting is likely to be a rarer event than the telephone meeting, but this makes in-person conversations that much more important. Stack the deck in your favor and ASK for the meeting. Your connection might be too busy, but chances are that he or she will feel flattered, particularly if you are seeking expertise from a position of genuine curiosity about this person's experience.

Introductions to Hiring Executives

Now recall the number of times you have been introduced by a connection, personally, to a hiring manager. Rarer still, these opportunities to meet actual hiring executives are precious chances for you to show the value you could bring to a company or an industry. Prepare for these meetings wisely—they are not likely to be frequent, so make the most of the chance to make that special first impression.

Job Interviews

Interview offers can come in cold, from the submission of your resume to an indifferent website or email, but they are more likely to develop because of your ongoing, powerful, and planned networking strategy. Therefore, this is the metric that matters most in your networking efforts. Bring your best game and use this opportunity to show how you are the right fit for the company.

Identify the Bottleneck

Where in this process did your numbers drop off? Was it at step 1? Maybe you are not putting yourself out there sufficiently at the broadest level to create as many new connections as you can. Was it at step 4? Why do you think hiring managers—those with the power to extend critical interview offers—are not following through? Not getting a second interview? Then you must examine your interviewing strategy for step 5. Wherever the bottleneck seems to reside, figure out why your experience has followed this pattern.

— 11 —

LINKEDIN

KEY REASONS FOR AN OPTIMIZED LINKEDIN PROFILE

LinkedIn is the world's largest free address book. If you are not on LinkedIn, you simply do not exist to recruiters and hiring executives, not to mention networking contacts that you need to maintain throughout your executive career.

LinkedIn Is Your Personal Page in the World's Largest Address Book

In all of social media, no single space has the professional clout of LinkedIn. You might have a Facebook page, Twitter account, or even a Pinterest page. However, if you are not on LinkedIn in a meaningful way, you simply do not exist online, professionally speaking. In fact, you diminish your credibility as an executive if you are not willing to create and maintain a LinkedIn profile that demonstrates experience and engagement in this social media network.

Recruiters and Hiring Executives Are Looking for an Executive like You

Studies have shown that upwards of 80 percent of recruiters and hiring leaders use social media to research their prospective hires. Most often, LinkedIn profiles appear in Google searches above any other content about an individual.

However, unlike most of the Google results, you have 100 percent control over what you put into your LinkedIn profile. You control your message and brand. If you are not dictating what the world learns about you in your LinkedIn profile, you are missing a tremendous opportunity to manage the conversation.

How to Quickly Add Content to Your LinkedIn Profile and Optimize It for Searchability and Content

Because LinkedIn is free and simple to use, there is no excuse for every executive not to have a robust LinkedIn profile. At a minimum, you need to include every title you have held for the last ten to twenty years, all listed separately, even if some represent promotions within one company and are stacked in one "job" together.

A more powerful strategy is to copy your resume into your LinkedIn profile, which will populate all of these positions. I do not recommend you do this if you have more time to put to the project, but it is an easy way to add valuable content to your LinkedIn profile. If you must take this approach, make sure that you are obscuring or deleting altogether any private business content you would not want to share with 700M+ across the globe.

A yet even more powerful strategy is to think about the top five keyword phrases on which you want to be found, or for which you want to be known. Then recraft your headline, your summary, and your career history to reflect this brand.

Additional key tip: If you do not have a professional photograph in your profile, add one right now. Research has demonstrated that profiles with recent, credible photos earn more profile views. Also, unlike your executive resume, there is an expectation that you will have a photo in your LinkedIn profile.

Outcomes for Your LinkedIn Presence

The result of your effort to optimize your LinkedIn presence for both searchability and for networking can be profound. On the one hand, you are controlling the message that the world learns about you even via a casual review of your online presence. On the other hand, you are more likely to have the opportunity to demonstrate your expertise, because you will appear closer to the top of the LinkedIn search results.

PROFILE KEYWORD STRATEGY

Do you know how to choose the right keywords for your LinkedIn profile? Start with your goals in mind: What do you want to be known for? What executive job are you seeking? With a few smart tweaks to your LinkedIn profile, you will see the number of your profile views grow.

Start with Knowing What You Stand For

Your brand will dictate most of what goes into your profile. Your LinkedIn profile will contain your career history. But the way you craft it and the keywords you choose can help propel your profile to the top of the search results for the phrases on which you want to be found.

Let us examine an example of a senior vice president and chief operating officer. This SVP/COO is known for his turnaround strategy and for his financial leadership. In fact, he functions more like the CFO of the company than the COO. So, his LinkedIn profile keywords will reflect his expertise. They might include:

- Senior vice president
- Chief operating officer
- Turnaround management
- Financial strategy

The details of what this person has done in his career will be much more extensive, but these are, broadly speaking, the categories of his expertise. He would be wise to include these phrases in his headline, his summary, and in his experience sections.

Continue with What Hiring Executives in Target Companies Need to See

At the same time, he might be targeting a COO role. So, he might collect several job descriptions of the COO role in his industry. These might require specific experience and expertise; his experience and branding should reflect exactly what the hiring executives in his target companies are seeking in their next hire. Although the LinkedIn profile is not a direct copy of the executive resume, elements of key experiences (less private corporate data that should never be publicized on LinkedIn) should be evident.

DO THESE TEN THINGS ON LINKEDIN RIGHT NOW— ALL IN LESS THAN ONE HOUR

You're thinking, "I definitely have an hour to spend, but I don't know how to use LinkedIn properly." The interface is complicated, and it's always changing, which makes keeping up even harder. I will tell you, however, that most executive job seekers don't know how to use LinkedIn well. Learning the best way to work with LinkedIn's various tools and capabilities definitely will move your executive job search forward.

To complicate things, if you don't keep up with all the different functions that LinkedIn offers, you might find yourself behind your competition to connect with the right people to find the right executive role.

If you're stressed about how to use LinkedIn for your job search presence, follow these ten simple daily strategies to target your talents and expertise to your executive ideal job search goal.

1. Connect with someone you don't know personally on LinkedIn and customize your connection request so they understand exactly why you've reached out to them.
2. Write a LinkedIn recommendation for someone else.
3. Call up a LinkedIn connection with whom you have not spoken in at least six months.

4. Look on LinkedIn's job board for interesting positions open right now.

5. Review several colleagues' profiles to see what they have been up to.

6. Join a LinkedIn group and post one question—or comment on someone else's question.

7. Take those business cards you collected from your last networking event and connect with each of them on LinkedIn.

8. Write a long-form blog post and publish it on LinkedIn.

9. Look at a LinkedIn company page to see when their next industry event or webinar will be held, then make time to participate.

10. Read an article in a publication related to your industry or job function. Then update your LinkedIn status with a link to it and a question or insight about it to your connections.

Can you do these in less than sixty minutes? Time yourself—you'll be surprised at how fast you can complete them. Know how to use LinkedIn well with these ten daily tips, and you'll master your executive job search.

WRITE A GREAT LINKEDIN HEADLINE

If you could rank LinkedIn profile headlines (the 120 characters that show up next to your photo in searches), which would be the *worst*?

A. A well-honed description of your job title, industry, and value-add.

B. Your job title alone.

C. Something on your "results-driven" attitude.

D. Your employment status.

If you're a savvy LinkedIn user, then your choice would be (D), including your employment status. Anything other than choice (A) will likely not get your profile the degree of play you hope, but let's focus on the biggest error that I see in LinkedIn all the time.

In the past, pre-COVID, I would have recommended that you think critically about what your LinkedIn profile is really telegraphing if you state outright that you are an executive searching for a new opportunity. You'll fall into one of two categories: If you're employed, then you're sending the wrong message to your existing employer and will probably hurt your chances for success with your current company. If you're unemployed, this is not the brand you want to promote—shouting from the rooftops that you're out of work leaves yourself open for bias at worst and benign neglect at best. Don't stonewall a potential lead with a sign that says, "do not enter." Lately, in the wake of the COVID crisis, however, many LinkedIn users are adding photo frames to their headshots that indicate they are "Open to Work," and some are using hashtags to show their availability as well. As the photo frame was implemented at the height of the pandemic, as of this writing it's hard to tell whether this particular implementation will have an impact on hiring trends. In both cases, I would not recommend putting anything about your employment status in your headline—this is not a brand, it's a description of your current state.

The 120 characters (more, if you're editing on the mobile app) provide your profile's billboard to the world, not to mention a critical opportunity to improve your profile's chances for being found on the words that describe your brand best. This is called search engine optimization (SEO), and many of the long-tail keyword strategies prevail on LinkedIn.

JOIN GROUPS TO BOOST YOUR RELEVANCE

Maximize your career opportunities through your membership in LinkedIn groups. Every member can join up to fifty main groups. Executive job seekers on LinkedIn want to be notable or found for the expertise they deliver. Although the official help source on the LinkedIn interface doesn't mention joining groups as a key to improving your search rank, it has been reported anecdotally that group membership matters.

CHOOSE THE RIGHT LINKEDIN GROUPS FOR YOUR EXECUTIVE JOB SEARCH

Pick LinkedIn groups that will promote you as an expert in your field.

1. Choose LinkedIn groups related to your job search target.
2. Choose LinkedIn groups related to your functional expertise.
3. Choose LinkedIn groups related to your field of interest or industry.

By relating your profile with those similar to you in interests, industry, or job title, LinkedIn is likely to believe that you are authentically part of these affinity groups. But this is just the start. Having groups on your profile is not enough to convince LinkedIn that you are part of these groups. While belonging to groups tells something about your authenticity and your brand, membership alone will not convince LinkedIn of your relevance.

You have to post topically relevant status updates regularly, in your timeline and in your groups. Engage other group members to create relevant, reciprocal, socially mediated engagement that is topically focused and related to your executive job search. Your posts and comments should relate to your job search target, your industry, and your job function.

KEY METRICS FOR YOUR LINKEDIN PROFILE

If you wonder what the point of engaging on LinkedIn might be, or how you determine the success of your profile, look at the metrics that LinkedIn provides. The breadth of your connections on LinkedIn is a good metric to evaluate, because you can see it grow as you engage on the social media platform. When you sign up for LinkedIn you have zero connections, and, depending on your strategy for engaging and building your online network, you can have one hundred connections, five hundred connections, or thousands—up to thirty thousand in total.

The Number of Connections You Have

Strategic Choices for Growing Your LinkedIn Network

Your LinkedIn connection strategy will determine the growth of your LinkedIn profile. Some people choose to guard their first-degree connections closely, only connecting with or accepting connections from people they know well. Taking the opposite view, some become LinkedIn LIONS (LinkedIn Open Networkers), accepting and seeking connections from anyone willing to introduce themselves. Whatever strategy you choose, LinkedIn itself recommends having a minimum of fifty first-degree contacts.

Benefits of Measuring Your LinkedIn Network Growth

The benefit of growing your first-degree connection list is you have resources on whom you can call for information when you are engaging in many business activities, including executive job search

The bigger benefit for you as you seek to advance your career is the exponential growth of second- and third-degree connections. These are the connections of your connections, perhaps individuals you'd never have the chance to meet otherwise, and they can serve as invaluable sources of insider information as you determine your career objectives, target companies, and executive job search strategy.

The Number of Times Your Profile Has Been Viewed

The number of times your profile has been viewed is a good proxy for the success of the level of your engagement on LinkedIn. When people read your updates and find them interesting, they'll click through your name to read your profile. Also, if your LinkedIn profile is well-populated with strategic keywords, you will earn profile click-throughs because your message resonates with the needs of hiring executives and recruiters.

Strategic Choices to Increase the Number of Your Profile Views

You can strategically increase your profile views in two key ways. First, share updates more frequently. These can be your own posts in the form of microblogging or from your regular blog. These are thought-provoking statements or questions about your industry or your knowledge about it. You can be a content curator and repost, "like," share, or comment on what other people have posted or published elsewhere. You don't have to be clever and original all the time—you simply have to commit to engaging your audience.

Benefits of Measuring the Number of Your Profile Views

It's beneficial to keep track of your profile views from week to week. It serves as an excellent measurement of your ability to engage well on a day-to-day basis. The more you post, share, and "like," the more people will come to expect a certain perspective or point of view from you related to your industry or executive position. These people will feel like they "know" you, want to learn more about you, view your profile, and, hopefully, engage with you in real time, which can only benefit you both.

ACCEPT (ALMOST ALL) LINKEDIN CONNECTIONREQUESTS

There are exponential benefits to accepting most of the LinkedIn requests that come your way, particularly if you are exploring executive career opportunities.

You might be open to accepting every connection—or no connections. Overall, your strategy for accepting and creating connections has to work for your specific situation, particularly if you are looking for work. Following is a quick test to determine whether to accept a LinkedIn connection request.

Is the Profile of an Actual Person?

There truly are LinkedIn "catfish" out there, so explore the person's profile before you accept a connection. You can do an image search on the person's photo to verify that the name and photo are connected elsewhere.

Is This Person a Connection of a First-Degree Connection of Yours?

Usually, you can trust that the connection of someone you know well is also a real person. Perhaps ask your first-degree connection about the request if that adds a layer of security.

Does This Person Belong to a LinkedIn Group in Which You Participate?

It is easy to request to connect with someone when you are both members of a LinkedIn group. The public group forum also opens opportunities for you to communicate with someone before accepting their requests.

Does This Person Have a Current or Past History at a Company That You Are Targeting for Your Executive Career?

If you have a mutual professional interest, you might have common ground to explore.

Does This Person Have a Connection to Someone You Need to Meet?

Although this is a rather mercenary reason to connect with someone, it is a no less valid reason to do so.

Does This Person Offer Insights or Updates in Other Social Media?

Note this person's other social media posts. Do you have reason to expect more of the same?

Can You Offer Anything of Value to This Person?

This person might ask you for a key piece of information or for access to your network. Are you willing to offer help?

Do You Know Someone Whom This Proposed Connection Should Meet?

You might see from this person's profile that he or she is targeting a company that you know well. If the connection seems sound and the individual seems earnest, you might offer to make a valuable connection on behalf of this person.

Note that not all of these tests reflect cost/benefit to you—some reflect ways you can help the individual who is reaching out to you. The only way to maximize the connections you have is to continue to grow your own list. Not all will be active, and you should not expect that all will be one-way connections in which you provide value and the requester takes all. The bottom line is for you to determine how you can contribute to a new relationship—both online and offline.

THE FIVE PEOPLE YOU NEED TO KNOW ON LINKEDIN

There are five people you need to know on LinkedIn to advance your executive job search. These are the people whose insights you will find helpful in the process of exploring new roles, interviewing, and evaluating job offers—but they are not who you think.

A Peer in Another Industry

So often, we connect on LinkedIn with our colleagues in our own company or in companies similar to ours. LinkedIn loves that we are part of a peer group, and the platform judges our relevance by the company we keep. However, as you search for a new role, explore outside your company and your industry to learn what others at your level do and believe. You'll uncover the parallels between your job and your peer's job and discover the gaps between what you do in your job and what a day in another industry might look like for the same role. This analysis will help you evaluate your own skill set and perhaps help you set your job search strategy if you do not want to stay in your current industry.

A Superior in Another Industry

Have you ever wished you had a fairy godparent who could advise you on something sensitive related to your career? This is your opportunity to find that mentor or trusted advisor. An executive in another industry may not know exactly how your company or division works, but this person, a trusted expert in his or her own industry, is likely to have some insight into the way things work. Make it clear in your request for ten minutes of this person's valuable time that you are not taking advantage of their position to get yourself a job in their company. With this ethical approach in mind, use these ten minutes to ask questions about your career advancement strategy and get advice from an impartial observer.

A Recruiter Specializing in Your Industry

Although your LinkedIn profile might not advertise that you are seeking a new executive role, perhaps to protect the position you have, connect with a specialized recruiter or two before you launch into job search mode. Identify which recruiters regularly place candidates in your industry and in your job function. Remember, the recruiters who place candidates in your existing company likely will not try to place you in another company as this is a breach of ethics. Instead, with some discreet inquiries or even a quick Google search, find the right recruiting firm and the right recruiter within that firm. Then send a brief, polite invitation via LinkedIn to connect with these one or two individuals. Remember, recruiters do not work with you—they work for the companies that pay fees for placing executives like yourself with unique skill sets, so mention in your introductory note exactly what your unique selling proposition is.

A Peer in a Company That Interests You

Your first thought in connecting with someone in a company that you are targeting might be the hiring executive himself/herself. Rather than initiating a relationship with a company with an implied request for a position, start by connecting with people at your level. They might have some unique insights into the way the company works. It is likely easier to make a friend with someone at your own level than someone who sits at a level far above yours. In time, this person might advocate for you based on the good relationship you have built.

The "Connector" in Any Industry

It might help to connect with a few LinkedIn LIONs or "connectors." These are people who seem to know everyone and have connections across industries and companies. They are outgoing and willing to make introductions. Set up a few minutes to talk to someone with these qualities once you have made that connection on LinkedIn. Ask whether this connector knows someone who can help you (you specify the criteria) and would make an introduction on LinkedIn, via email, or in person.

Remember, LinkedIn is only the tool. Set up the relationships on LinkedIn long before you need them for your particular executive job search. When you are ready to start looking for a new job actively, these credible connections that you have already established will be extremely helpful and valuable to you.

THIRD-DEGREE CONNECTIONS MATTER

How many first-degree connections do you have on LinkedIn? Forty? One hundred? Five hundred? Ten thousand? The thirty-thousand limit that LinkedIn currently imposes? That figure shows the number of people you have influenced to join your inner circle. But it's not indicative of the power of your influence overall on LinkedIn. The most powerful number on LinkedIn is your total third-degree LinkedIn connections.

What Are Third-Degree LinkedIn Connections?

Before we talk about the value of these third-degree connections, let's define what we mean. Imagine you're standing in a circle that contains only you. Everyone with whom you're connected directly is your first-degree connections. Now imagine one of those first-degree connections standing in his or her own circle; everyone to whom that person is connected (unless they are also your first-degree connections as well) is your second-degree connections.

Example: You are connected to Mary. Mary is connected to Joe, Tom, Jack, and Jane. Joe, Tom, Jack, and Jane are your second-degree connections (assuming they're not also first-degree connections of yours).

Now imagine that Joe is standing in his own circle. He has first-degree connections, too. These individuals are your third-degree connections (unless they're more closely connected to you in some other way).

Example: Joe, Tom, Jack, and Jane (your second-degree connections) also have pools of first-degree connections. This entire set of connections-of-your-connections'-connections comprises your third-degree connections.

What Happens to Your LinkedIn Connections When You Connect with Someone New?

Your inner circle is only as large as it is; you can expand it via several techniques, and you definitely should do so as you progress through your executive job search. When you add a first-degree connection, your second-degree circle expands, but your third-degree circle grows exponentially. When one of your second-degree connections adds a new member to his or her inner circle, your third-degree pool also grows. Consider that LinkedIn had 706+ million users in 2020 in over two hundred countries and territories worldwide, up from 450 million in 2018. Thus, the number of connections in your broadest circle is growing exponentially, even while you sleep, even when you are not active on the platform.

Why Third-Degree LinkedIn Connections Matter for Your Job Search

Third-degree connections matter because no relationship activity valuable to you specifically happens outside of your network. In practical terms, this means that you can't know about someone's participation on the platform if you do not share some relationship (connections being only one flavor, but the most powerful and reciprocal).

From a search standpoint, all search results on the platform are dictated by relationship status. When a hiring executive looking for someone like you conducts a search (using the regular LinkedIn membership level, not the recruiter membership), their results will include only those who are first-, second-, or third-degree connected. This means that a hiring executive cannot find you unless you are part of that person's extended network. You simply will not appear in the search results for that individual. You won't be on that person's radar, and if you're not in the differential, you won't be in the diagnosis—if you're not in the pool of candidates, there is no way you can be chosen even for initial evaluation of candidacy.

How to Build Essential Third-Degree Connections

The number of third-degree connections you have is largely out of your control. However, if most LinkedIn users abide by roughly the same principles, every new connection that you make or someone else makes deepens and strengthens all levels of connections. To actively increase the number of third-degree connections you have, start by connecting with individuals whose brand is a hub on LinkedIn. These individuals are called LinkedIn Open Networkers, or LIONs. Search these LIONs out by region, industry, job function, or company, and connect with them; most do not reject connection requests.

BECOMING A LION: BALANCING THE PROS AND CONS

If you are you proud of the number of connections you have on LinkedIn, it's a metric you wish to cultivate, and you definitively explain the value of having a thousand connections, consider becoming a LION.

We all know that special person who just "knows everyone." When we have a question about something specific, we ask that person for a contact, and he or she just pulls one up, having built a Rolodex of the right people. This is the "connector" who can help us find the right resources. LIONs are willing to serve as a connecting hub for hundreds, if not thousands of LinkedIn connections.

The value of becoming a LION is clear. The more people with whom you are connected on LinkedIn, the more likely you are to have a connection who has a connection in a company of interest to you. So, if this is true, why shouldn't everyone seek to build a LinkedIn connection cast of thousands?

The pros of becoming a LinkedIn LION also are clear. By announcing your status change, you'll be inundated with connection requests of perhaps hundreds. Accept them all. Watch your profile views grow radically from week to week. Post interesting status updates along the way, and you'll likely see your posts circulate widely.

On the other hand, you won't really know these new connections, unless you make a practice of getting to know each one. What is likely to happen is that people will connect with you specifically because they want access to your network, which is easy on LinkedIn but harder if not impossible in real life. How can you recommend the expertise of someone you don't know to someone you don't know?

Thus, if you're a numbers wonk and just want to see your metrics change, by all means, become a LION. Announce your new position on all the groups to which you belong. Put it in your headline. Ask for connections and state that you'll never give an "I don't know this person" response to a request.

However, if you are a serious job seeker, you'll see pretty quickly that LION status is just that—a status. It doesn't have a qualitative impact on the strategy of your job search. Instead, keep building your network strategically. If that means that along the way you reach out to a LION—in your industry, in your job function, or known to someone you know well—to access strategically that person's network, then do so. But don't dilute the value of the connections among those who trust your discernment by thinning out your network beyond strategic need.

You can walk the fine line between both of these possibilities in your job search without committing to either one.

Using the above recommendation about growing your connections to increase your third-degree circle through existing LIONs, find a LION (perhaps two or three) who bear characteristics that are interesting to you. I recommend that you do a search for *"LION + your industry + your targeted job title + recruiter."* This will reveal a list of people who are LIONs already and are waiting for more connections to accept, who are interested in or aligned to your industry and job function, and who are recruiters. You might choose to tweak your search criteria, adding parameters such as city or state, or changing up the job function or industry, until you have reached out to two or three LIONs. When they accept your connection, your second-degree circle (hence your third-degree circle) will have instantaneously grown.

On the flip side, feel free to accept connections that don't seem sketchy but who aren't necessarily an intimate of your current social circle. You're effectively functioning as a LION, with some limitations and boundaries, without advertising you are doing so. Take this strategy for a test run and connect with me on LinkedIn at https://linkedin.com/in/amyladler. In your connection request, let me know you saw my invitation here!

WHY YOUR PROFILE IS NOT YOUR RESUME

Your Resume Will Be Your LinkedIn Profile, If LinkedIn Has Anything to Say about It

There is significant buzz about LinkedIn being the forum of choice when looking for work. We know recruiters use it to source candidates; what about job seekers using it as their job application "app" of choice?

If we assume that conventional online job search systems can be inefficient, frustrating, and a barrier to finding good placements, we can be confident that there are lots of openings to make the system better, easier, and more efficient for both sides of the hiring process.

LinkedIn Has Stepped In to Fix This Problem

LinkedIn has developed an app that dumps your profile into a pretty resume template, which users can save for downloading. At the same time, employers can now use an "apply with LinkedIn" button on their websites. These ease the burden on the part of the applicant and the employer to get applications in quickly.

Regardless of whether candidates plan to use their profiles as their resumes, LinkedIn clearly hopes they will. However, I don't believe they've solved the critical requirement of resume customization per job target—profiles remain static unless job seekers tweak their public presence every time they apply for a new position.

LinkedIn Is NOT Your Resume

It can't be. Not yet. LinkedIn is so flexible that it can't serve as a resume that a job candidate can use to apply for every position worth applying for. The following criticisms of the process have been raised:

1. The templates that LinkedIn offers for resumes are pretty, but they use space inefficiently and are highly standardized; you might determine that your unique career situation demands a personalized resume style (I'm sure your resume writer would agree to this point without question).

2. Although users can create multiple versions of their resume and export them to PDF or save them in the system, each new resume targeted to a new position requires a live tweak of the profile. We all know that once a user hits "save" on a

profile, the profile is live—there is no "holding space" for multiple profile versions. Job seekers would have to save their multiple profile versions on their desktops in Word or Notepad.

3. Resumes and cover letters should be customized for each job-search target. If a job seeker were to tweak their profile for every position, the world would see new versions of that person's candidacy every time he or she applied for a new position. To me, that's just confusing.

4. There is no cover letter option on LinkedIn. Because some hiring managers like them and some hate them, smart job seekers should include them. Enough said.

5. HR departments are likely to be flooded with untargeted applications. With the ease of applying in place, candidates could apply everywhere, regardless of their actual qualifications, endlessly flooding human resources departments with resumes and placing a significant burden on HR to identify viable applicants. There would have to be additional gatekeeper questions by companies to eliminate the needless flood.

6. Hiring managers need to know MORE about candidates, not the SAME information as presented on a resume. The profile is a candidate's prime opportunity to demonstrate why he or she is unique, capable, and a good fit, using more than simple accomplishment statements. The rules are looser compared to those governing the stringent requirements of the resume. Candidates should take advantage of these open opportunities to enhance their online image.

Is LinkedIn the Promise for the Future of Online Job Applications?

I think we all rather hope so. If there was a one-touch option for applying for multiple jobs, the process would be spectacularly easier and efficient for applicants and effective for the companies seeking them. But as it stands, resumes and LinkedIn profiles are different, and they have different audiences. Knowing when to use which is key.

PROTECT YOUR PROFILE

LinkedIn and Microsoft Word Resume Assistant

Normally, when you adjust your privacy settings, you're selecting the audience you want to see your LinkedIn profile. But there is one LinkedIn setting that you will want to select to ensure that LinkedIn doesn't share your content.

When Microsoft purchased LinkedIn in 2016, it included a feature in Microsoft Word that enables LinkedIn members drafting their resumes to update their profiles and discover and apply for jobs on LinkedIn. While it has always been possible to view profiles of individuals in similar roles for inspiration when constructing your resume, LinkedIn headline, and profile content, this extra feature allows users to copy directly content from other peoples' LinkedIn profiles. And, in fact, it is encouraged by Microsoft and LinkedIn.

Fortunately, LinkedIn also added a new privacy setting to allow you to omit your LinkedIn profile from showing up in Word's Resume Assistant. Disabling the sharing function makes it harder for others to plagiarize your content—whether you wrote it yourself or had help from a professional resume writer.

Here's how to turn on the LinkedIn privacy setting to disable Resume Assistant. When logged into your desktop LinkedIn account:

1. Click "Me."

2. Click "Settings & Privacy."

3. Click "Privacy."

4. Scroll down to the "How others see your profile and network information" section.

5. Click on "Microsoft Word."

6. The default setting is "Yes" — "Allow Microsoft Word to display work experience descriptions from your profile to users of Resume Assistant." Changing the setting to "No" keeps LinkedIn from sharing your descriptions with Microsoft Word users.

7. Slide from the default "Yes" so it shows "No."

You can also change this setting in the LinkedIn mobile app. In the app, go to the "Settings" gear in the upper right-hand corner and click "Privacy." Scroll down to "Microsoft Word" and display the setting. Change the slider to "No."

When "Resume Assistant" is enabled, it shows what other people in similar roles say about themselves in their LinkedIn profiles, allowing users of the word processing software to incorporate that content directly into the resume they are creating (with their legal permission but not their ethical permission). The big question you have to answer is whether you want to copy others' approaches—good, bad, or unique to them—or to be a wise, unique executive with nothing to copy from anyone, nor with anything copyable. Simply stated, are you one of the million, or one in a million? Smart job seekers undoubtedly choose the latter.

PART 4

APPLY

— 12 —

THE TACTICAL SEARCH

APPLY FOR ONLY SIX JOBS

"Why am I not getting interviews?" you're wondering. "I'm sending out dozens of resumes, but the calls aren't coming in."

When job search candidates tell me they have applied for hundreds of positions and received no interviews, they usually sound panicked and angry. After all, with all that effort they are putting into their job searches, why aren't they getting any interviews? They are baffled, frustrated, and worried about their chances for success. They don't see that there are only perhaps six jobs that are right for them.

The first thing I advise these frustrated executive job search candidates is to stop applying right away. The strategy they have chosen is not working—they're not getting positive responses to their resumes, and they are not getting interviews that match their expertise. There is something very wrong with their approach and doing more of it will result only in more frustration and fewer calls for interviews.

There Are Only Six Positions

Then I ask what positions they are targeting. The wide range of responses is staggering. And this is the problem. There are no "hundreds of positions" that are right for any one person—no wonder there are no calls for interviews. I would posit that there are only six (or thereabouts) positions right for any single executive. So when executives are frustrated because they are not getting interviews, I tell them it's because they're casting a net that is by far too wide.

By eliminating all positions and companies that are not directly in the bulls-eye of your job search, paradoxically, your job search will become more fruitful. You'll target your entire job search process to this set of positions, which you have taken time to identify, focus on, and target your messaging toward. Yes, it might feel like you're eliminating hundreds of possibilities, but instead, your message is becoming more authentic and more believable to your hiring entity. You'll start to sound like the executive they have been looking for all along.

So how do you focus on your six ideal jobs? You leave out everything that's not in your ideal zone. If the job does not target:

- Your values
- Your corporate culture
- Your function
- Your growth
- Your aptitude
- Your skill set

Then do not apply and have zero regrets about leaving it off your list.

STOP SCOURING ONLINE JOB BOARDS

If you're looking for your next executive job on online boards such as Monster and Indeed, you've got a lot of searching, reading, filtering, and applying to do. Every day, you have to log in, search, read, filter, and apply . . . and then do it all again the next day.

Have you done this? Have you felt the frustration that comes with doing all of this for perhaps hours per day with few positive results?

The reason you feel like you're getting small bang for your buck is that online job boards, particularly for executives, are not effective for job search strategy—in isolation. You might feel you're doing a lot—all that search/read/filter/apply can take hours of your day. But the return you can expect from doing all of this will be slender.

How You Should Use Online Job Boards

First, stop applying (if you are) to dozens or even hundreds of jobs. This requires a significant shift in your thinking if it has been your sole strategy to date. Instead, use the big job boards and the specialty job boards to get a sense of what hiring executives typically want candidates to address when they apply for positions. Think about the skills, knowledge, and abilities that these roles require, and start mapping your resume strategy to them.

Second, set up job search alerts on each job board and on Google Alerts. Alerts send you daily updates of positions that match the criteria you specify directly to your email. Now all you need to do is check your email one time per day to see whether any of the positions mentioned are good prospects for your executive job search. You'll save hours that you can now use more strategically.

What to Do Instead

You might feel you're not doing anything if you give up your daily scouring of the online job boards. It will feel very different from your prior practice, but you'll soon see the benefits of your efficiency. Use the time you've opened up to build the relationships that will get you into target companies before they post a position. For example, if Smith, Inc. is a company of interest, and you believe you'd make a great General Manager there, then start researching the company. Read its website. Google its press releases. Learn about its products or services. Then, look on LinkedIn to see whether you know anyone who works there, or whether you have a second-degree connection who works there. Now take that connection to the next level and see about getting the right introduction for an informational interview. You'll be surprised at how successful your in-person, humanized executive job search strategy can be.

THE INFORMATIONAL INTERVIEW: WHAT IT IS, WHAT IT ISN'T, AND HOW TO DO IT

People hire people, not resumes. So, you need to be a person before you're a resume—to engage with individuals who can support your candidacy. You need to do informational interviews. Even if you're a senior executive with twenty-plus years' experience in your field and industry, you need to set up, strategize for, and do informational interviews. Your job search might fail without this critical job search strategy.

Informational Interviews: Not Your Grandfather's Job Search

If you're frustrated with your job search, I'd be willing to bet that your strategy included at least one of the following:

1. Reading job boards, tailoring your resume to each position, and sending it out.
2. Skimming companies' career websites and uploading your resume.
3. Generating a list of companies and sending it out to "Dear Sir or Madam."

There is a better way, and you can do it: The informational interview.

This Is Not an Informational Interview

"Hi, thanks for speaking with me today/having me here today. I'd like to tell you about my experience, assets, and abilities, because I'm looking for a job. Do you have a job for me? If not, do you know who is hiring? And furthermore, if you look at my resume [hands over resume], where do you think I fit in your company?"
Tone: Desperate.
Content: Me-centered.
Only possible outcome: "Sorry, I am not hiring now."
Subtext: I'm looking for a job.

This Is an Informational Interview

"Hi, thanks for speaking with me today/having me here today. I have heard so much about your company/product/service, and I'm truly curious about the processes and people that go into producing it. How did you get into the role you currently have?"
Tone: Curious and interested.
Content: Outwardly focused.

Only possible outcome: "Sure, let me tell you how I was hired here. I originally went to school for X, but I wound up doing Y. I've been in this company 15 years . . ."
Subtext: I'm looking for a job.

That's a good start to an informational interview. It focuses on what the audience can offer about his or her experience and asks open-ended questions, none of which are "Will you hire me?" Of course, the subtext in any informational interview is that the candidate is in a job search, but that's not really the focus of the discussion; it hovers in the background, but it's not at the center of the discussion. The center of the discussion, then, is the person with whom you're speaking. Give them the platform, be authentically curious, and learn from them.

How to Engage in an Effective Informational Interview

Overall, informational interviews are not actually interviews. They are not about you, the candidate. Informational interviews are opportunities for you to ask questions and learn. Informational interviews are not only for new college grads; they can be useful for senior executives as well. They might be formal in-office conversations, or they might be brief phone calls. Either way, they are targeted discussions about the individual with whom you're speaking and the company.

Get ready for your informational interviews

Prepare:

Learn as much as you can about a handful of individuals with whom you wish to speak.

Secure meetings:

Ask for ten minutes on their calendars; follow up in a week if you do not receive a response. Move on from those unwilling or unable to fit you into their busy schedules.

Ask open-ended questions:

How do these people interest you? What do they know that you don't? What drives them to go to work every day?

Capitalize on the connection:

Who do they know that you might benefit from knowing (and vice versa)? Are they willing to make an introduction?

Follow up:

Thank the individual at the end of the call or meeting. Send a follow-up thank you, expressing gratitude and referring to the action steps the person agreed to take on your behalf, if any.

Reach out to recommended connections:

Start the process over; fairly soon, you'll have added dozens of people to your personal informational interview pipeline.

Service Orientation for Your Informational Interviews

Remember, informational interviews are two-way streets. Be service-focused and give as much as you take (or ask for). Be a helpful resource in any way you can for the individual with whom you're speaking.

COOL TOOLS TO SEARCH FOR JOBS ONLINE

If you are spending more than 10 percent of your time searching online for jobs, you are wasting your time. Put the internet to work for you—get job alerts and company information emailed directly to your inbox. Use these cool tools to automate the search process, so you can focus on networking into the right role.

Monitor Social Media Channels with IFTT

Setup an application called IFTT (If This Then That) to send you an email whenever you are mentioned on Twitter. Sign up for a free account at http://ifttt.com/. Browse and use recipes for pre-made monitoring, such as:

- Sending an email alert when your target company is mentioned in The New York Times

- Sending an email alert when your name is mentioned on Google+

- Track all new Twitter followers
- Email tomorrow's weather, so you know whether to bring an umbrella to your interviews
- Create an Evernote page with saved hashtag searches on Twitter
- And anything else that you need to know or can think of. Be as creative and detailed as you need to be to monitor your online presence effectively

Set Up Google Alerts

Sign into your Google account and visit google.com/alerts. Use your name as the search query and determine what information you want to be searched:

- Everything, News, Blogs, Video, Discussions, Book
- How often you want to receive email alerts
- How broad you want the results to be (Everything, Only the Best Results)
- Where you want the alerts sent

Now select the phrases that you want to monitor:

- Your name
- The name of an executive with whom you hope to interview
- The names of companies you are targeting
- Industry topics of interest
- And anything else that you need to know to enhance your job search

Some tips:

- Using quotation marks results in these sample search results
- Removing the quote marks makes it more likely that you will receive irrelevant results
- You can modify these alerts at any time, so start with broad results, and you can refine them over time

Set Up Alerts from Job Boards

Let Indeed.com, Glassdoor.com, Monster.com, Dice.com, and LinkedIn do the legwork for you. These automated alerts (sometimes called "agents" or "saved searches") will generate the results you need without your having to visit each site every day. Because you should be spending more time on human connections than on scouring the job boards, this is an easy method to ensure you don't miss an excellent opportunity without committing endless time to the process.

Now select the phrases you want to monitor:

- Job title
- Geographical region
- Industry
- Job characteristics
- And any other specifics of your target job that you want to know about

USE A CUSTOMER RELATIONSHIP MANAGEMENT TOOL

Your job search is like a business, and if you are not leading your pursuit as well as you lead your business, then you are losing critical opportunities. Successful businesses use customer relationship management (CRM) tools to manage their pipelines; use a CRM to manage your job hunt pipeline, saving time, effort, and confusion.

Using a CRM for Your Job Search Saves You Time

All CRMs organize information slightly differently. However, the hallmarks of the system include a robust contact management system and the ability to assign a set of related tasks, with target dates of completion, to particular individuals or companies. You can easily customize those tasks for a job search. For example, you can set:

- Dates of initial contact
- Dates interim follow-up
- Dates of planned telephone interviews
- Dates of planned face-to-face interviews

Choose milestones important to your job search, just the way your sales team appoints milestones for your company's sales pipeline.

Using a CRM for Your Job Search Saves You Effort

Who do you need to contact today? What do you need to ask that second-degree connection on LinkedIn?

Your CRM is your virtual memory jog to help you remember exactly what you need to tell each person on your list each day. Your search for the right email address or phone number is over, and you no longer have to stick Post-its to your monitor to remind you of what you need to accomplish.

Using a CRM for Your Job Search Saves You Confusion

What do you do when you are out and about, or at your desk, and the phone rings? Let's suppose this is a contact you need to reestablish—or even a target company on your short list. Are you ready at a moment's notice to engage properly with a caller? When you have all your executive job search information in a CRM, quickly search on the caller's name or company, and you will have the information you need.

There are many good reasons to use a CRM for your executive job search. In fact, some CRMs are designed specifically for job search, such as JibberJobber, but you also can use a more generic one and customize it to your needs. Many commercial CRMs have very good free options that you can upgrade as you build your list and as your needs increase.

— 13 —

WORKING WITH RECRUITERS

RECRUITERS DO NOT WORK WITH JOB SEEKERS

HAVE YOU CONSIDERED sending your resume to one or more recruiters to help find you a job? Recruiters are exceptional professionals who know their markets well. They know how to research a company, identify its needs, and present several candidates who they believe have the right assets and approach to fulfill that company's expectations. And they are paid by the company doing the hiring. You, as the executive job seeker, do not hire the recruiter to work for you, and you do not pay the recruiter. Thus, your needs, wants, and expectations do not play strongly into the way a recruiter does his or her work until you are a powerfully viable candidate.

Recruiters Are Paid by the Company Seeking to Hire

Recruiters receive their fees from companies when they agree to hire a candidate. This means they do not work for you and they have no obligation to help an individual who is considering a job change. Rather, recruiters are more likely to follow the money and position candidates who they believe will be hired, which then translates into their earning a fee for placement faster. Successful candidates show they can uniquely fulfill a hiring executive's needs. And this is the rub if your skills and assets are marketable but, frankly, fairly common.

Unique versus Average

The best candidates are at the top of their game, currently working, and have a skill set uncommon in the marketplace. These candidates are more difficult to find, and they certainly are not throwing their resume around to every company and every recruiter in the industry. If they are looking for a new role at all, they are doing so discreetly and privately. These candidates are extremely valuable to companies; hence, they are extremely valuable to recruiters, who could receive top fees for placing candidates in roles with highly specialized requirements.

The rest of the candidates in the pool have fairly common skills and are not likely to be those whom companies will pay fees to hire. In terms of simple economics, the supply of these individuals meets or exceeds the demand, driving the price (the recruiter's fee) downward, perhaps asymptotic to zero.

You Can Win Either Way

Whether your skill set is entirely unique or the work you do is more common, you can take advantage of this knowledge about the way recruiters think and work.

First, know that a smart recruiter will find you if your skills are sufficiently out of the ordinary, and they need to fill a company position requiring someone just like you. If you are approached out of the blue by a recruiter who knows of a role to be filled, absolutely take him or her up on the opportunity to learn more about the position.

If you are considering giving your resume to recruiters in the hope they'll find you a job, stop right there. Recruiters are not likely to take the time or energy to position candidates for roles for which there are hundreds of viable candidates—companies simply will not pay the fee for talent they could easily scoop up on their own. And if a company rejects your candidacy because you presented via a recruiter (whose fee would be owed several months beyond the initial introduction had you been hired), it might not have the privilege of hiring you without the attendant fee for quite some time.

Therefore, take control of your job search and don't assume a recruiter will do your heavy lifting. Create a target list of companies you want to investigate and become the first point of contact on your own. When the company sees your candidacy does not come with a 15–30 percent price tag, they might look twice at your highly marketable assets.

ETIQUETTE TIPS FOR WORKING WITH RECRUITERS

One of the biggest questions I frequently receive is how best to "work" with recruiters. As part of a well-rounded career search strategy, working with recruiters can be extremely valuable. If you choose to work with a recruiter, or one seeks you out, follow these top etiquette tips to ensure a smooth, positive, mutually rewarding relationship.

Be Responsive to Inquiries

Speed is one of the most critical factors when working with a recruiting firm, especially contingency recruiters. If a recruiter is trying to reach you to discuss an opportunity, he or she will want to talk to you right away and will likely move on to someone else if you are hard to reach. You might get a second phone line that you use only during your job search and an email that you use only for your job search. If you have a standard Gmail address of firstnamelastname@gmail.com, you also can sign up for a free or low-cost redirecting phone number that rings to an existing number of your choosing, such as your mobile phone.

Be Respectful of Your Recruiter's Time

Remember, too, that recruiters often work on numerous search assignments simultaneously. Many recruiting firms require a minimum number of successful placements each month for the recruiter to keep his or her job. Consequently, be mindful of the recruiter's time when you make contact. Need to have a partner and guide through the process? Hire a career coach or resume writer instead—this type of professional will be devoted to your specific case.

Build a Relationship

As a general rule, always take a recruiter's call, even if you are not looking for a new position. A recruiter in your industry can provide valuable information and help you shape your own career path. Don't treat conversations as transactions. You'd hate being treated that way and so do recruiters.

Be Findable on LinkedIn

Recruiters know how to find candidates, even the ones who are working in jobs they love. However, you can make their jobs easier by publishing a robust LinkedIn profile, joining relevant industry or function-related groups, building a powerful LinkedIn network, and ensuring your profile is set to public viewing. LinkedIn has several job seeker features that can help you be more visible, such as the #OpenToWork tag or photo frame that lets viewers know you're open to inquiries as well.

Be a Valuable Networking Contact

You can be an excellent source of information for the recruiter. Keep your eyes and ears open for opportunities and candidates and share that information with them. If you are not a fit for an opportunity, but you can recommend someone else, share that information. A recruiter will remember that you provided a new contact for him or her when the opportunity was not exactly right for you and will think of you the next time.

Be Specific about Your Career Requirements

When you're looking for a position, be up front with the recruiter about the work, company, salary expectations, and so on that you need to explore opportunities further. The recruiter's goal is to fill open positions, so the more information you can provide about your non-negotiables and on what you will compromise, the less likely you will be to frustrate a recruiter who has worked very hard on your behalf in positioning you to the wrong company.

Know that You Are Not the Right Candidate for Every Recruiter

Don't contact too many recruiters—especially at the same firm. Recruiters often have access to an internal candidate management system that allows them to see what contact you've had with other recruiters within the firm and other positions you've applied for.

Be Up Front about Your Recruiter Relationships

Let your recruiter know when you are actively working with another recruiter. If two contingency recruiters submit you as a candidate to the same firm, the client company may not consider you at all, even if you are a perfect match. Companies don't want to mediate an argument between recruiters about who "owns" the candidate (and who would receive the commission if the successful placement is made).

Recall How Recruiters Earn Their Fees

If you are working with a recruiter, don't apply for the same positions you are being submitted to as a candidate. You may inadvertently disqualify yourself because the employer won't risk having a recruiter claim a commission if you are hired directly. If you see a position advertised and are contacted by a recruiter for the same opportunity, decide whether you want to apply directly or be submitted as a candidate by the recruiter. Even if you have a networking contact at the company, you may determine that a good recruiter can get you in front of a hiring manager more easily than you could get noticed yourself. This is particularly true if the employer uses an applicant tracking system to screen resumes; recruiters can often reach hiring managers directly.

Be a Compelling Candidate

Last, but certainly not least, develop a compelling professional brand. Show in your executive resume and your LinkedIn profile that you are rarely and uniquely suited for hard-to-fill roles so recruiters choose you for the unusual skill set you bring to the employment marketplace. While you will not automatically fall off recruiters' radar for being average, you are more likely to capture a busy recruiter's attention if you can demonstrate the scarce skills and assets that a hiring executive demands.

— 14 —

THE INTERVIEW

THERE IS NO SUCH THING AS "NOT PART OF THE INTERVIEW"

LET ME TELL YOU a very personal story. Two decades ago, when I had just finished a master's degree program, I was in job-search mode. I had achieved an interview for a job I was interested in and was sitting before the hiring executive. He asked me all the usual interview questions, which I answered to the best of my ability. He also asked me something tangential, I believe about my master's thesis and the way I did the data analysis. He postscripted this question with "This is not part of the interview." Without thinking, I knee-jerk responded with, "There is no such thing as 'not part of the interview.'" I suppose I also answered the question about the data analysis. I didn't get that job—in fact, I got another one elsewhere for which I was much better suited. But I never did forget, and I have repeated many times, that there is no such thing as not part of the interview.

When you are applying for an executive position, you'll go through many interviews. You'll interview with executive boards, CEOs, CTOs, CMOs, potential colleagues, and even subordinates. You walk through the company's hallways, you'll sit at desks, in conference rooms, in lobbies, and maybe even in restaurants. None of these locations are private, and none of the people with whom you interview are obligated to remain quiet about your conversations. Even if your executive interviewer suggests that your conversation will remain private, he or she has no obligation to remain circumspect about what you say. In fact, the more inflammatory your comments are, the more likely someone will repeat them in the form of gossip about your level of professionalism or in the form of a polite letter declining to take your candidacy further.

Thus, it makes sense for you to measure every word and sentence that you utter, not only from the perspective of your executive accomplishments and your executive role but also by the dimensions of whether you are comfortable with your words being repeated by people you don't know well to people you don't know at all. Here are a few guidelines for you as you move through your executive interview:

1. Treat everyone you meet professionally, including administrative personnel. You might even earn some goodwill points by writing a quick email to the receptionist to thank him or her for the kindness shown to you on the day of your interview.

2. Do not let your guard down during your interview, no matter how comfortable you feel with the interviewer. This might be especially true if you know one of the panel members well. That person is not your friend in this context: That person is testing you the same way he or she is testing every other candidate who's interviewed.

3. If you are uncomfortable with even a legal question, be prepared to either a) answer the question asked or b) respectfully decline to answer based on its level of appropriateness. If you answer an illegal question, you open up a tremendous can of worms and the opportunity for your interviewer to probe the issue more deeply.

As an executive in an executive interview, you are on stage and being evaluated at every turn. Anything you do can and certainly will be used against you. By monitoring your behavior and behaving like the professional executive that you are, you can avoid being caught saying something you can't defend or doing something you wish you hadn't. Remember: There is no such thing as "not part of the interview." With that caveat, it's time to celebrate your success thus far and ready yourself to nail the interview.

PREPARE FOR YOUR INTERVIEW SUCCESS

Congratulations! All of your hard work has paid off—you got the call! Now you need to prepare for a successful and smooth interview.

Research the Company Broadly

Researching a company is critical to having a successful encounter with the hiring agent. You need to walk into the interview with confidence.

- Check the website. You'll discover a tremendous amount of useful information about a company's financial health, recent news, and community involvement. Learn what the company's values, missions, and goals are.
- Check with your network. See what your partners know about the company—both pros and cons.
- If possible, talk to current and past employees—check out the work environment.
- Learn who the competitors are and what impact they have on the company.
- Research local business journals, national news, databases, and more. Learn whether the company is growing or contracting, if it has recently launched new products, or if it has received an influx of investment money—this can tell you a great deal about the company's current trajectory.
- Research the company's top employees on LinkedIn.

As you prepare for the interview, keep in mind that you are not just learning about the company and its culture, you are learning about the people they hire. Through this type of research, you are developing your own presentation plan on how to handle the interview itself.

Narrow Your Research

- Review your information and target key areas that you may want to discuss during the interview.

- Determine how your strengths can help the company move forward and achieve its goals.

- Create talking points that you can use to discuss the company's unique values.

- Be prepared to explain how hiring you will benefit the company.

- Develop questions to ask during the interview. Show your interest in the company. Don't be afraid to ask about future goals of the company.

- Use LinkedIn and Google to look up the name of the interviewer. Learning names and titles can help you feel more comfortable during the interview. Check to see if you have any common interests.

The more that you learn about a company prior to an interview, the more confident you will be going into the interview itself. You will have an idea ahead of time if you are a good fit for the company culture.

Prepare Your Story

Put yourself in control by being prepared and showing your positive attitude and insightful knowledge about your experiences and expertise.

- Study your resume and practice your answers in front of a mirror or camera so you can retell key points of your career history relevant to the position you're seeking. Practice answering the hard questions: "Why were you terminated?" and "Tell me about yourself" are perhaps the two most difficult, but these can be interview killers if you do not prepare ahead of time with answers that succinctly address the question and focus on the future.

- Clean up your social media. Many companies will search your social media prior to hiring to look for red flags—items that can cause you to lose that spot in the hiring lineup. Be ruthless and eliminate posts that may cause concern to potential hiring managers.

- Look the part. You need to be perceived as a member of the team and as someone who can fit in with the company's culture. Whether the environment is business casual or office professional, you need to know how to present yourself. You won't go wrong by dressing up, even for a semi-casual environment; you can always hang your jacket on the back of your chair if everyone else is in T-shirts, but you'll never dress up a golf shirt if everyone else is in suits and ties.

INTERVIEW PERSUASIVELY

In our day-to-day lives, we all want to be humble and modest, but being self-deprecating won't give your prospective employer that lasting impression or memorable interview that you are going for. An interview is a time to get out there and shine. You need to sell yourself; be persuasive without coming across as over-confident or arrogant.

The power of persuasion will become second nature the more you use it. Don't be afraid to speak passionately and from the heart. Emotions are powerful; just don't go overboard or talk too fast. It is always wise to be somewhat in tune with the interviewer. However, being around someone enthusiastic and positive can be contagious. Let them feel your energy and zest for life; it is bound to leave a good impression and persuade them to give you a chance.

Get Out of Your Comfort Zone

Push yourself; allow yourself to brag a little. Put your selling points on the table. Don't take it too far, but don't be afraid. This is why you are here, to show them who you are and what you are made of. Don't be shy; jump at the chance to shine. You want to paint them a glorious picture of what you have to offer so that the image and information stay with them. To be persuasive, use details that can be felt, seen, and tested—visualized and remembered—including numbers to prove your points. You can use metaphors or an analogy if you are cautious. Remember, this type of persuasive detail may be hard to come up with on the spot. Plan ahead and develop examples. Be ready.

Demonstrate Credibility

Aspiring employees are often hired based on who the interviewer feels can get the job done. They need to count on you; they must trust you. This begins with believing what you say in an interview. To strengthen your credibility, you must sell or demonstrate your expertise and build a positive relationship or connection with the interviewer. Find common interests. It could be a geographical location, hobbies, or feeling the same way about issues in your field. Don't be afraid to ask about your interviewer's experiences with work or to talk about life outside of work. This creates a feeling of a conversation more than just another interview. Showing expertise may be as simple as being aware of the current trends in your industry.

Your message should show your potential contribution to the company based on your company research, reflecting your audience, not you. What would this person need to know about the ways you can solve the problems he is facing right this minute? You should have a good sense of what these issues might be based on the research you have completed prior to your interview. If you do not know specifically what the key problems this particular executive is facing, ask what issues keep this person up at night. You might be surprised by the person's candor, and this can spark a complex conversation in which you can offer your own brand of potential solution.

Stick to the Facts

Don't launch into an awkward monologue about yourself full of your own thought and opinions. Instead, state some objective facts to highlight some of your accomplishments. Talk about awards you have received, stats you have improved, anything that is concrete.

Give Yourself Some Credit; You Are Not a Novice

If you are just getting started in a particular field, don't make statements about getting your feet wet or just starting out. Even if you are changing industries, every bit of experience counts. Most occupations have certain things in common—it may be sales, customer service, or a creative touch. You may have done something in your past experience that will benefit you in this new position, even outside of your work history. Plan ahead and be ready to use persuasive examples to highlight your legitimate skills and traits. You may not have been "paid" for a particular skill, but it could still be useful in your future employment.

Quote Others Who Have Seen You in Action

Discussing statements that others have made about you is a great alternative to bragging. It sounds better to say something like, "I was recently told by my manager that he has really seen the results of my project development skills." A statement like this can be very persuasive if done properly.

Toot Your Own Horn

Most of us aren't good at talking about ourselves, let alone tooting our own horn or convincing others to have confidence in our abilities. Keep in mind that an interview differs from any other interaction. You must make an impression. You have such a limited amount of time for them to learn about you that you must make every minute count. Don't miss out on a position you are qualified for due to your unwillingness to level with your audience. Tell them the facts of the case, what you did, and how you solved the problem, letting them know as much of the outcome of your actions as you can. Show the right level of pride without overdoing it, and you'll find that you'll bring your interviewer into your story effectively and with the right amount of compelling emotion.

Practice

Selling yourself may seem difficult, but with practice it can become nearly automatic in an interview situation. Always be authentic and remember to be truthful. There is a big difference in speaking of tried-and-true talents and experience versus selling false ideas. This will always come back to bite you. Be interesting and concise when speaking of your strengths and what you bring to the table. In practicing and speaking out loud, you will hear where you need to make changes and avoid any awkwardness. You aren't rehearsing a speech; your answers should vary slightly each time, with key points and information staying the same.

Don't Wait

Once you have your selling points and have practiced your presentations, jump in and interview. Don't let too much time go by before using the skills you have been working so hard on. Be proactive and seek out opportunities to continue to practice.

Keep the Lines of Communication Open

Particularly when you have been invited to continue the discussion, keep the lines of communication with your interviewing team open. If you see something interesting in the news that might be relevant to the needs of this future hiring executive, pass it along with a brief note. Follow this person on LinkedIn and other key social media in which this hiring team participates. Every now and then, "like" or retweet their posts or comment on them in a relevant way. Most important, do not neglect to send quick thank-you letters to each of your interview team within twenty-four hours of your interview, preferably not before the sun goes down on the day of your interview. Highlight your value and add anything else about your candidacy that you believe will support your value.

PRACTICING YOUR PITCH

Nobody Has Time to Listen Anymore

If I am right, you barely have time to read this book. You're busy, you've got work to do. I respect that. Hiring executives have the same problem. They don't have any spare time, either. So, as you approach the executives who can help you throughout your job search, you'll come up against their time crunches. You have to convince them that you're worth putting their calendar on hold for.

Knowing what you do about busy executives—after all, you're a busy executive yourself—how do you make this meeting easy for your contact? You keep it brief, at least until you're challenged to expand on the assets you bring and the accomplishments you've demonstrated. if you can't tell who you are and why you are relevant to a listener's needs, you have failed. You have failed to make yourself memorable, and you have failed to explain why you are taking the valuable time of your new contact.

"Hello. Nice to meet you. Why don't you tell me about yourself?"

This is the deadliest question, and your answer can make or break your interview—almost before it starts. The more succinct you are in answering, the more likely you will be called on for additional details. Therefore, you need to prepare this message, your mission, and your value proposition ahead of time—long before you get the question—because they *will* ask you.

To develop your core message or so-called elevator pitch, explore the following:

How do you label yourself?

Tell me who you are in ten seconds or less. Alternatively, tell me who you are in three bullets. I know that this is a tough exercise, particularly the first time you try it, but I'm confident that you'll hone it to perfection in plenty of time for that important interview or networking event. Consider the answers to the following questions, which might help you uncover your core message:

1. What is your current job title?

2. What do you aspire to do?

3. In what industry do you aspire to do it?

4. What is your noble purpose?

5. What is a representative example of the type of contribution you make?

Are you getting closer to the ten-second mark? I will bet that you are.

How would others label you?

If you're still stuck for a self-description, imagine what your executive leader, your co-workers, or your subordinates might say about you. For example, are you:

1. Compassionate?

2. Visionary?

3. Technologically savvy?

Have you reached the ten-second mark? If so, job well done. Now you need to practice it. I heard one theatre coach suggest that an actor doesn't really remember his lines until he can recite them while doing jumping jacks. While I don't suggest that you either play a part or prepare yourself in a cardiovascular sense, the premise remains a logical one. You should be able to recite your ten-second pitch in any context, under any circumstances, with confidence, strong inflection, and a smile.

Take some time to practice. If you're still struggling about what to say or how to say it, you can always ask for help from a career coach or executive resume writer. After all, "I'm a career-brand strategist for executives and their teams."

WINNING THE INTERVIEW GAME

What if you could get inside the minds of the top leaders about their hiring decisions and strategy? Given that the interview is inherently designed to screen you out, the better you can assess the hiring leaders' styles and their needs, the better your chances are of meeting them where they are in their decision-making processes.

LinkedIn provided insight into this strategy with a blog series called *How I Hire*. This captured what influential hiring leaders in the strongest companies believed to be essential about their specific hiring processes. Let's take apart a few of their comments so you can assess your interviewer's style and needs.

Time Frame to Assessment

What the Interviewee Thinks: When will they decide what they think of me?

What the Interviewer Thinks: At what point in the process do I know this is the right or wrong person?

Interviewee Solution: As the interviewee you might not know much about your interviewers' personalities ahead of time, so you need to assess them as quickly as they are assessing you. Are they quick to ask you deep questions about your level of commitment, or are they asking all kinds of seemingly disconnected questions? This can help you decide if the interviewer is a go-with-the-gut rapid decision maker or someone who needs a dozen or more data points to come to a solid conclusion.

Intangibles Essential for Each New Hire

What the Interviewee Thinks: I have the technical expertise.

What the Interviewer Thinks: I need a culture fit.

Interviewee Solution: Do your research, but not only on the company's product or service. Learn about current employees to figure out what makes the company unique from a cultural point of view. Read its mission and values statements. Find out where its employees volunteer their time. Learn what personality characteristics are vital for success in this company. Your answers to questions about your own personality and culture profile might stand up nicely to others interviewing for the same role.

Being the Part—If That's Really Who You Are

What the Interviewee Thinks: I've got to be my best because I need this job.

What the Interviewer Thinks: I need someone whose core personality fits my company and the specific role.

Interviewee Solution: Be yourself. The interview is your time to shine—or be instantly screened out. Influential hiring leaders surveyed for this LinkedIn series agreed they have preconceived notions about what a person should do/be like/project—and it's up to them to fill the position appropriately. While you should know the needs of the role and the corporate culture, you also need to be true to yourself. If you don't fit at the beginning, don't force a round peg into a square hole. Neither you nor your hiring leader will be happy.

INTERVIEW MISTAKES THAT WILL SABOTAGE YOUR CHANCES

If you're interviewing for a new position, you might accidentally give your interviewer simple reasons to reject your candidacy, even if you are the most qualified for the role. Here are five interview mistakes that might damage your chances for hire—and easy tactics to avoid trapping yourself in poor interview behavior.

Letting Your Present Job Get in The Way of Your Future Career

If you truly hate your current job, you might inadvertently convey your frustration to your interviewer. For example, how do you answer the common interview question, "Why do you want to leave your current position or company?" Your response should not include the reasons you don't like your current role, as anything you say about your former company will reflect poorly on you.

Try this: Demonstrate that this company is the right fit for you *moving forward* because your interests and abilities clearly align with its needs.

Not Knowing the Company's Product

Prepare for each interview by learning as much as you can about the company's products or services. Read industry websites, learn about the department's staff on LinkedIn, and download the company's white papers. If you have specific questions about emerging technology, new markets, or product variations, ask your interviewer for some insights. However, if you get into an interview and do not understand what the company's core products or services are, you will reveal yourself to be uncommitted and not worthy of a second interview.

Try this: Learn not only about the products but also *how the company's best customers use them effectively*.

Being a Know-It-All

There is nobody more knowledgeable about your experience and history than you are, and during your job interview you should be prepared to explain the ways your experience can benefit the company directly, based on your exhaustive company research. However, you are not yet an expert on the inner workings and needs of your interviewer's company. Crossing the line from interested interviewee to overbearing know-it-all can be insulting to your interviewer and might ruin your chances for a second interview.

Try this: Ask honestly and engagingly about something you want to know—never assume you know better than the interviewer.

Dressing as if a Company's Casual Culture Applies to You

So many companies tout their worker-friendly, casual atmospheres. While this can be a draw for many who prefer a relaxed over a structured environment, these rules do not apply to you as the interviewee. For men and women, a professional dress code applies regardless of what you might know about how the company's employees regularly dress. Even if you are instructed to dress casually, it's always better to dress professionally.

Try this: Use the "grandmother" test: If your grandmother (or your future boss's boss) would not approve of your ensemble, then do not wear it to your interview. See below for a few recommendations on how to prepare your wardrobe for interview day.

Believing That You Are Not Being Watched

Again, there is no such thing as "not part of the interview." Every person with whom you speak, from the interviewer, to his boss, to the receptionist, is watching you and evaluating you. If you are kind to each person with whom you interact, your behavior will speak volumes for you, but one demeaning comment can destroy your candidacy.

Try this: Write down the name of *every* person with whom you interact so you might write a brief note of thanks for their help throughout your interview day.

BODY LANGUAGE FOR YOUR TELEPHONE INTERVIEW

"Hey, wait a minute!" I hear you thinking. "A telephone interview is just that—an interview over the telephone. The interviewer can't possibly see my body language." Nevertheless, a good interviewer can *hear* your body language. If you don't present yourself in a telephone interview exactly how you would present yourself in person, your interviewer will hear your hesitation and instantly put your resume in the rejection pile.

When you schedule a telephone interview, select a time and location in which you won't be distracted by work, family, or other competing interests for the duration of your interview. Even small disruptions can clue your interviewer that you're not focusing 100 percent on your interview. The face-to-face equivalent is revealing in your facial expression that your chair is uncomfortable, that you don't like an odor in the air, or something else that steals your attention away from critical focus.

Another body language habit that you should avoid in a telephone interview is putting your hands to your face. In an in-person interview, such behavior can convey that you don't quite believe your own words, which undermines your expertise and command of subject matter. On the phone, putting your hands to your face can muffle your voice or pull the receiver away from your mouth. Any additional interference to mobile and VoIP connections that are already dicey can prevent your interviewer from concentrating on your answers to the questions.

Although you would never stand during an in-person interview around a desk or conference table, consider standing while speaking during your telephone interview. Standing while you speak has a few advantages over sitting. First, standing with proper posture opens your chest, enabling you to speak comfortably for long periods. Second, and perhaps more importantly, standing while conversing on the phone might be uncommon for you, meaning you'll focus more on the conversation and be at the top of your game more than you would have been sitting or slouching in your chair.

Finally, pick something to focus your eyes on. During a face-to-face interview, you'd focus on the people around the table. This body language forces you to focus on the interview and keep your attention where it needs to be. During a phone interview, you don't have a person to look at, so pick an object, something in the room that holds your attention without being so detailed that examining it takes you away from the topic, and use that as a focal point. Although you're standing, you won't be able to pace and distract yourself. Instead, you'll be listening carefully and ignoring competing visual cues.

PRESENTATION FOR YOUR VIDEO INTERVIEW

Even before the COVID crisis, some companies were moving to virtual interviews. Video interviewing companies, such as HireVue boast platforms that are designed to manage interviews virtually. However, with the advent of COVID and its associated reduction in travel and uptick in virtual video meetings, it is wise for candidates to know and implement best practices for video interviewing. Of note, these are not altogether different from best practices for video meetings plus telephone interviewing strategies.

Prepare Your Technology

Most laptops and phones have video cameras built into their technologies. Many desktop computers require external web cameras. You must have one or the other to connect effectively with your interviewing team.

Prepare Your Station

When you know the app that your interviewing team plans to use (ask early if you don't), test it out with a trusted friend or colleague, and set up the layout of your chair, desk, and technology properly. Ensure that your head and upper body are centered appropriately on the screen and that you are not craning your neck (or huddling over your device) to see the camera or your screen properly.

Prepare Your Background

As an addition to the above, be mindful of what others might see behind your chair. Best practices include using a blank or minimally decorated wall and well-lit space. If neither of these is possible, try the virtual background options within your technology—many programs have dedicated tools for this. If your computer is slightly older or if its video capabilities are not virtual-background-ready, you can buy and hang an actual green screen, easily purchased online. Using your technology's green screen option (often with the addition of a nifty free app called ChromaCam) will help your audience see you, not your messy office shelves.

Prepare Your Cohabitants

Treat your interview space as sacrosanct and help those sharing your space to do the same. Prepare them in advance for the need for quiet, and close doors between you and them if possible.

Prepare Yourself

Dress fully as if you were preparing for a face-to-face meeting. You might stand up and inadvertently reveal that you are wearing a suit coat plus sweatpants.

CRACKING THE OFFICE DRESS CODE

Speaking of dressing for a professional interaction, recently I visited a very professional company. Imagine the reception I would have received if I showed up in jeans! Have you ever felt underdressed and unprepared for your job or your interview? Don't make this mistake in your job, and certainly don't make this mistake in your interview.

Dressing confidently for your job or your job interview can make the difference in the way you present yourself. Knowing the right way to dress professionally improves your presentation and your confidence, which, of course, can make all the difference in your interview. Retailer T. M. Lewin advises the following:

Business formal

Always dress business formal for interviews. Use your best judgment for including subtle pops of personality.

Women

- Trouser suit or conservative-length skirt suit in a neutral, dark color
- White-collared dress shirt
- Modest accessories
- Dark/Neutral tights
- Neutral-colored closed-toe heels

Men

- Two- or three-piece suit in neutral/dark color
- White or plain formal shirt
- Solid-colored unflashy tie
- Cufflinks or a watch
- Black or brown Oxford shoes

Business Professional

Avoid dressing more than one level up from your office dress code to avoid being overdressed.

Women

- Conservative-length skirt in modest colors
- Solid-colored top or blouse
- Dark or nude tights
- Neutral-colored closed-toe heels
- Modest statement accessories

Men

- Dark-colored suits in subtle, conservative patterns
- Pressed suit trousers paired with a matching jacket
- Brightly colored or conservatively patterned ties

Business Casual

Even if you work from home, dress as you would in the office to help shift your mind into work mode. Also, you never know when you might have to hop on a video call.

Women

- Skirt or suit trousers
- Shirts, sweaters, or blouses in solid colors or subtle patterns
- More casual statement jewelry
- Closed-toe heels, flats, or loafers in any color

Men

- Formal shirts in any color
- Sweaters or cardigans worn with collared shirts
- Ties are optional; most colors
- Suit trousers or chinos

Small Business Casual

Only dress one level down on designated "casual" days.

Women

- Suit trousers or knee-length skirts in casual fabrics like cotton or dark denim
- Shirts, cardigans or blouses in a variety of colors and patterns
- Open-toed heels, flats, sandals, or wedges
- Most jewelry

Men

- Casual chinos or trousers—no jeans unless explicitly stated
- If denim is okay, stick to dark colors and straight-legged styles
- Collared polos or crew-neck jumpers in most colors and patterns
- Clean and well-kept trainers or loafers

Creative

Take note of the majority of employee outfits when getting an office tour or going in for an interview.

Women

- Clean, wrinkle-free shirts
- Pops of color and unexpected patterns
- Stylish shoes or accessories that display personality

Men

- Specific niche dress codes will depend on established office environment
- Trendy fashion items and layers
- Tailored denim

FINISH THE INTERVIEW BY THANKING THE INTERVIEWING TEAM

You know you're the right person for the job and you think you gave all the right answers during your interview. You're pretty sure they're going to call you back with the job offer. You think you're done with the interview process, but you're wrong. You forgot to send each member of the hiring committee a post-interview thank-you letter.

Witness these recent statistics. Robert Half reports that only 5 percent of job seekers send thank you letters after their interviews. The Society for Human Resource Management (SHRM) adds to this—their study said 88 percent of hiring managers report that thank you letters influence their hiring decision.

So does this mean that 5 percent of the job seeking population has a leg up on the majority of interviewers who simply aren't playing by the rules? When you acknowledge an interview with a post-interview thank you letter, you have a huge opportunity to accomplish three tasks.

1. You thank the committee, individually, for their time. Until you are hired, you're simply a liability in terms of the amount of time and effort that it takes to get you on board.

2. You respond to the interview process, emphasizing how you can solve the hiring committee's pain beginning on your first day at work.

3. You tell the hiring executive that you want the job. Remember, we don't get what we don't ask for, so make sure that you are 100 percent clear about your enthusiasm for the role.

If you are not accomplishing these three goals in your post-interview thank you letter, you're failing to participate in a critical aspect of the interview process. In fact, you might have lost the chance to reiterate your interest in the position or to add to the data you provided in your interview. Make sure you send an individualized, well-conceived, thoughtful thank you letter to every member of your interviewing committee—it's an investment in time and effort that you will not regret.

CONCLUSION

MEASURE YOUR SUCCESS BY THE OFFERS YOU REJECT

IF YOU'RE CHALLENGING YOURSELF to find the right opportunity, you're hoping the next application you submit will result in a job offer. Then you can get out of the job you're in and into something new. Something different. Something... better?

Will any position do? "Yes," you are thinking right now. "I'll do anything, as long as it's not what I've been doing." If this is your thought process, borne of desperation, change it right now.

When executives are working steadily toward advancing their careers, they often view the job search as a numbers game—the more resumes they send out, the more interviews they theoretically should get, and the more competing offers they should receive. However, this thought process is faulty and doesn't take into account the executive's brand or corporate need. Nor does it account for the simple fact that not every job is right for a particular executive, and a particular executive isn't right for every job.

I receive a lot of comments from executives who report they need to get away from what they're doing. They're willing to take almost any position, as long as it's with some other company.

Running toward the right position never struck them as a strategy, given the high level of stress and frustration they were trying to escape every single day. They were taking interviews and would take offers from all comers. In fact, they might even have measured their success by the number of interview offers they received.

Can you imagine how these executives might feel in a year or two if they chose one of those offers just because it came from a different company? Probably, they'd feel the same level of frustration and disillusionment they were experiencing in their former role. Wouldn't you feel the same if you took a new position out of desperation, only to find out in a year that it was a terrible fit for you?

Your Metric for Career Search Success: The Number of Offers You Turn Down

Look at your own pattern of executive career search. Count up the number of interviews you've received. If you had received an offer from 100 percent of those interviews, how many would you have accepted?

Now think about your experiences critically. Do you truly believe that each of those roles was right for you? Why or why not? How many of those interviews or job offers would you have consciously chosen to reject? Perhaps you never thought about it that way, and this is exactly my point. You should be even more particular about choosing not to accept an interview than you should be about choosing to take part in one. If you know from the start that a company or role would never meet your needs, however you define them, then don't waste your time or that of the interviewer.

What does the number of offers for interviews or jobs that you reject tell you about your strategy? Why is this metric critical to your overall success? It shows you are evaluating future roles on their own merits, not because the prospective position is not your current one. Yes, it's hard to walk away from a process during which you've pursued a company and the company has pursued you. Being wanted is a heady thing. But when you reject a seemingly well-placed offer, you telegraph that you value your brand. You refuse to compromise on the value you can offer a company. You don't let yourself be drawn into a role that predicts the wrong future for your career. And you preserve the mental space and time in your calendar that will enable you to seek and achieve the executive role that is appropriate to your needs and aspirations.